PI

A Self-Study Guide on Becoming a Private Detective

Roger J. Willard, P.I.

PALADIN PRESS • BOULDER, COLORADO

PI: A Self-Study Guide on Becoming a Private Detective
by Roger J. Willard, P.I.

Copyright © 1997 by Roger J. Willard

ISBN 0-87364-954-0
Printed in the United States of America

Published by Paladin Press, a division of
Paladin Enterprises, Inc.
Gunbarrel Tech Center
7077 Winchester Circle
Boulder, Colorado 80301 USA
+1.303.443.7250

Direct inquiries and/or orders to the above address.

PALADIN, PALADIN PRESS, and the "horse head" design
are trademarks belonging to Paladin Enterprises and
registered in the United States Patent and Trademark Office.

Visit our Web site at www.paladin-press.com

CONTENTS

CHAPTER ONE   A Beginning   1

CHAPTER TWO   Requirements for Becoming a PI   9

CHAPTER THREE   Get Ready   17

CHAPTER FOUR   Your Private Office   25

CHAPTER FIVE   Field Equipment   39

CHAPTER SIX   Reports   51

CHAPTER SEVEN   Photography and Video   57

CHAPTER EIGHT   Firearms   69

CHAPTER NINE   Image   79

CHAPTER TEN   Where Do Clients Come From?   87

CHAPTER ELEVEN   Don'ts   95

CONCLUSION: My Personal Message to You   103

APPENDIX: Licensing Agencies and Requirements   105

RESOURCES   115

DEDICATION

In memory of my father, Howard L. Willard, and in honor of my mother, Adeline M. Willard, I dedicate this book. They were partners in business and in their lives together. Under one roof I learned that quality of service and quality of life go hand in hand.

Dad's work as a gunsmith was known throughout the area. What he gave was always more than he ever charged. From simple repairs to customizing stocks, he always did his best. His reward was not only a following of loyal customers, but countless friends—friends who would join him later in the evenings in picking banjos and strumming guitars. There was even a mandolin or two. But, more importantly, when necessary there was a firm hand to either guide and educate us or correct us when we went astray.

Mom was always there for him and the three sons whom they raised. She shared in the care of customers and at the same time made time for preparing meals, chauffeuring, and all those special events in our lives. She took care of all the store's paperwork and then checked our schoolwork. She has always been outgoing and able to carry on a conversation with anyone, anywhere. She now shares herself with six grandchildren as well, all of whom love her dearly.

To Mom and Dad, with love.

A VERY SPECIAL THANKS

Nothing I ever do, whether it be as a private detective, writer, speaker, or father, would amount to anything if I was not first Patti's husband. In whatever I do, she has a part or has inspired me in some way. Again, she has put in countless hours of proofreading and checking for grammatical errors in this, my second book. It would not have been possible without her. So, to Patti, as before and always, all my love and thank you.

ACKNOWLEDGMENTS

Over the past 15 years, I have come to know countless other private detectives. There is a select group, though, whom I call my friends. In sharing work, I have learned from them, and, I hope, they may have learned a little from me. Listing their first names here is my humble way of saying thanks. It also allows them to deny that they were the ones I meant and that they even know me. So, my thanks to Bob, Charlie, Chuck, Dan, Dick, Jimmy, John, Lanxton, Roger (the other one), Skip, and Shirley.

WARNING

Let the apprentice beware! Because laws and the way laws are interpreted by the courts change constantly, nothing in this book should be considered legal advice. It is the responsibility of the reader to confirm what may or may not be legal in his or her own jurisdictions. What may be legal in one place may be illegal in another. Therefore, please be forewarned that at no time does the author, publisher, or distributors of this book condone or promote any illegal or wrongful activity or provide any legal advice with regard to any of the information contained in this book.

CHAPTER ONE

A BEGINNING

From the age of about 13 on, I knew that I wanted to be a detective. I wasn't sure whether I'd be a police or private detective, but I knew I would be one or the other. I'd watch all the police and detective shows on television and imagine myself in the roles. When I graduated from high school, I learned that the process for becoming a police officer was pretty straightforward: you applied with various towns and cities and waited for a vacancy to come up. How to become a private investigator was not so clear, however. There wasn't a lot of information in the library on careers in private investigation, so I had to do a lot of research on my own. It took me a lot of time and effort just learning what it would take to get started in the field. That's why I wrote this book: so other people could learn how to prepare to become a private eye without having to do all the leg work that I did.

In the following pages you will embark on a journey of discovery. You will learn what you must do to prepare yourself for the craft of private investigation. You will be guided through what you have to do to get a license and start working as a private detective. You will be shown what is necessary to set up an office and keep it operating. A lot of what you will learn will come through work or research on your part. Doing this work, though, will be more rewarding than just reading about it in this or any other book. As you progress, you will discover what opportunities are available to you as a private detective and what the income potential is. You will see the good, the bad, and the ugly sides of this work.

Before you set out to explore this career path, the first thing you must learn and remember is that just about everything in your life that means something to you or has value to you is the result of your having set a goal. Consciously or subconsciously, you planned and executed a strategy for attaining all the things of value in your life.

I want each and every reader to understand that *you* set the limitations on your own life. You are the one in control of your life. Even when you feel that events, people, obligations, jobs, family, education, finances, or other surrounding circumstances prevent you from reaching or becoming what you want and need to be, you are wrong. But this is not to say that it is easy. It's not. It is hard work. It requires a substantial amount of thinking. And it will cost you something. This cost may be giving up some time with those you love. Your next vacation may be to the lake instead of Hawaii. You may have to put in some overtime at work so that you can afford to go back to school and then give up your evenings going to night school. But most of these costs are temporary.

Now here will be something strange for some people to comprehend, and that is that the journey is just as important as the goal. As you progress through this course of study, sometimes it will be hard, and for some it will be unpleasant. But when you see where it is taking you, you will be willing to tolerate these unpleasant times to reach the end of this course. At other times, as you go along you will find yourself very pleased upon having completed an assignment and in seeing what you have learned. The journey itself is many times its own reward.

This point is just as valid when applied to your whole life. Think about having a job that you hate but keep just because it pays you enough to do a few of the things you like to do on the weekends. Think now about this going on for the rest of your life. From Monday to Friday, all you would think about

2

was getting off work at the end of the week. Every Monday morning would be the worst day of your life. Eventually, even Sunday nights would start looking bad because you would know that the next day you would have to return to a job you hated. Not much of a life, is it?

Now think of having a job in which you are doing something that stimulates your interest, challenges you to be a little better every day, and rewards you with knowing that not only do you do the job well but you are recognized for it and rewarded accordingly. Think of having a job that makes you look forward to Monday mornings. Think of having a job that you do not even think of as a job but as something you like to do that you just happen to be paid well for. Would that not be a great job?

Yes, this job will require you to work, but you will not think of it as work. It may make you do things at times that are unpleasant, but you will find yourself doing them without complaining. At times, this job will make you sweat, but still you will look forward to the workout. This job will even cause you pain, but the overall pleasure and sense of achievement that you receive will quickly anesthetize it.

Your work, job, or chosen vocation is a major part of your journey through life. For some of you, the road you are going to take will be long and hard. For others, it will be a very short journey. Your goal is to become a private detective. Throughout this book you will learn how to find out what is required to become a PI. That is your true destination on your goal map. Your routes are the things you must do to meet those requirements. They may include an education, work experience or an apprenticeship, related training, relocating to an area that has a need for private detectives, purchasing equipment, and probably most importantly, perseverance.

Create and implement a realistic plan that puts you under some pressure to get there. Look for a challenge to get to your intermediate destination, demanding a little more from yourself than you normally do.

Think back to a time when you did do something that you were proud of—something you really wanted to do and do well. Literally, go back in your memory and try to re-experience the feeling you had when you were working on this project. Was there something you did to motivate yourself when you began to slow down? What mental exercises did you use to keep you moving? Your answers are what you are going to use to help you find the things that will motivate you on this new journey. Ask yourself these questions and see if there are similar things you can do to motivate yourself to take the necessary action.

Your motivator could be something you tell yourself, something you see or hear, or something else you do to put yourself in the frame of mind to set you on your path. Your motivator may be similar to those of others in some way, yet the particulars will be unique to you. Your motivator may be money, and there is nothing wrong with that, as long as it is a motivator and not an obsession. The point is, you will have to find something that keeps you on the path, because there will be times when you will tend to stray or wander and lose sight of your goal.

Be forewarned: do not let yourself become too content with yourself along your journey. Complacency is a motivational killer. There will be times to enjoy your successes—times to sit back and rest for a short while and enjoy the view of where you are at the time. But do not let yourself become seduced by this contentment. You will be tempted to stay in one spot too long and possibly forget where you were going. You may even be tempted to be satisfied with only going so far. At this point, your journey will have ended prematurely. Do not let it happen to you. You will regret it later. Enjoy your achievements, but remember that there are more ahead with greater pleasures and rewards.

As you take the first step of your journey by reading this book, you will note that I use words and terms that may or may not be familiar to you, and I may even drop a name or two—not to impress you, but to spark your interest and make you want to do a bit of research on your own. If you want to be an investigator, you must learn not only to ask questions but where to go or whom to ask to get the answers. This personal quest for information on your part will help make you not just a good investigator but a better educated person all around. In the end, even if you do not become a licensed private detective, you will have grown as a person; you will learn more about yourself and what you really want to do.

Before I go any further, I should try to clarify my use of the terms "private detective" and "private investigator." Throughout this book I will use them interchangeably. To me, and most people, they mean the same thing. In many law books, both terms are used to define the same person, that is, a private citizen with no police powers who is licensed to conduct investigations for hire. To be even more specific, this person is hired for money or reward or retained even when no money or reward is promised. He or she is a business person whose business happens to be investigations.

Some people and some legal jurisdictions are very specific in their use of the terms investigator and detective. To some, the term detective may only be used to describe someone with police powers. In another jurisdiction, it may have a broader definition. Even within the private detective community, there is some disagreement as to which term is proper for our profession. But again, in this book the terms private detective and private investigator will be used interchangeably. Only as a personal observation do I make any distinction between the two. This is that the term private investigator indicates to the public a more modern concept of the profession, whereas the term private detective conjures up images of characters in the old black-and-white movies out of the 1940s (such as Sam Spade in *The Maltese Falcon*), and the more romantic, adventurous view of the work. As I will discuss later, this perceptual distinction may affect the way you will want to promote yourself, your profession, and the kind of work you want to do.

So now that you've decided to venture into the world of the private detective, let's get started.

I recommend that you get a notebook, because you will want to take and keep notes. You will want to have a record of some of the information that you will be getting on your own. Several folders with pockets might be helpful for keeping anything that you might want to photocopy.

At the end of this and most of the remaining chapters you will find assignments. There may be one or several for you to do. No one will be looking over your shoulder and making you do them, of course, but in doing them on your own, you will begin your practical training in becoming a PI. If you have not already learned to be self-motivated or disciplined, now is the time. As a PI you will have to decide when and how much work you will put into any project you do. In doing the assignments voluntarily, you will learn the true meaning of perseverance and self-discipline. That said, let's get started with the first one.

ASSIGNMENTS

1. Write, in one sentence only, why you want to become a private investigator. Be brief and yet reveal your true inner feelings about why you want to do this kind of work.

_____

_____

_____

_____

_____

2. On a 3" x 5" file card, write down a very specific goal. Do you want to have a private detective agency? What kind of investigations do you want to do? Do you want to work for an agency and not have to worry about the headaches of owning an agency?

3. On additional cards, write down some possible requirements (intermediate points) you expect you will have to fulfill in order to attain your goal (e.g., school, experience, meeting people, going places, physical preparedness).

4. Arrange the cards in order from where you are now to where you want to be.

5. Add a date to each of the steps. Create a timetable.

6. As you read this book, occasionally review your list of steps to see if any new ones can be added. Add them if necessary. Subsequently, delete ones that are no longer necessary.

7. As described earlier, try to ascertain what motivates you and write it down. Be as specific as possible.

8. Take a survey among the successful people you know. Ask five of them if they were lucky or if they took action to make their own luck and reach their goals.

CHAPTER TWO

REQUIREMENTS FOR BECOMING A PI

Next to having a big eye painted on the window or door, what tells a client that you are a PI? In most states, it is having a license on display in your office. How and where to get a license are the pertinent questions at this point in your training. First, you must understand that there is not a nationwide license for PIs. States have their own procedures and criteria for obtaining licenses, and some require no licensing at all. Many states have a state licensing board as well as local licensing agencies. In some states you might obtain a license through your local police department or county court.

Requirements also vary from state to state. In some states, having a certain number of years in law enforcement is a prerequisite. Others require an internship or no experience at all. About 10 years ago I heard of a junior high school student who got his own PI license (he lived in a state that had no age requirement). Being a little older now, I can see that life would have been much more difficult for my parents had I known when I was his age that certain states had no minimum age requirement. I would have tried anything to get them to move.

In a number of states there are different levels of licensing. In these states an individual may obtain a license to work as an investigator for an agency, but not on his own. They require an agency license or an investigator/agency license to open a private investigation business, and yet another license or combination license to provide security services.

The real point here is that you have to check with the state in which you'd like to become a PI to find out the licensing requirements. Another point to consider is that these laws are not stagnant. What I tell you about your state law may have been true when this book was printed, but it may have changed by the time you read it. There are several books in print that list the licensing laws for every state, and some are very good and as up-to-date as they can be. These books are good if you want a general outline of what is required in each state. Other books I have seen are very inaccurate. I usually use my home state to test the accuracy of these books. If it did not get mine right, it probably did not get the rest right either.

So, where does this leave you, the Sam Spade in training? It depends on what you plan on doing and how old you are. Because this book is also intended for the younger person, I will explain what you may want to do if you are too young to get a license or meet the necessary qualifications to work as a PI. First, let me say that in no way do I suggest that you should violate any laws or do anything else illegal, but as a minor, you are given some latitude in what we will call, for now, "playing detective." As long as you are not operating a business for which you are being paid or interfering with any legitimate investigation or any other legal process, you may be permitted to "play detective." This means looking into minor matters locally, doing research, checking public records, and operating a small office so that you can learn what the work is like.

If you are 18 or older, forget what I just said. You can still do most of the things mentioned in this book, except for actually taking on cases for other people. You may do work for yourself, but you still would not be able to call yourself a PI. There is nothing wrong with learning this way, and you can still have some fun doing it, but again, in no way should you violate the local laws as they apply to PIs.

So what do you do to become a legitimate PI? First, you have to research all the applicable state and local laws. To do this, you have to decide whether you want to work for an established agency or open your own. If you choose the former, you need to find out the licensing requirements in your state. If you choose the latter, there may also be laws pertaining to the operation of a business in general that apply, as well as on where you may locate your business (zoning). To research these laws, the best place to start would probably be your local library. Call or visit and ask if it has a law library. If so, let your search begin there. If not, ask the librarian if he or she knows whether your county has a public law library. If so, that would be your next stop. If neither is close by, you may have to try a surrounding city or county. Your local bar association may also be able to help you.

If there is nothing close by and you do not have the means to travel far, you can call a library that does have what you want, such as your state library. Ask what it would cost to make photocopies of any and all laws governing the licensing of private detectives in your state. Then send them a letter requesting this information along with whatever payment is required. In your letter, make note of the person you spoke to or whomever you were instructed to direct your request to. Addressing the letter "to the attention of" that person on the envelope and at the top of the letter will help ensure that it is directed properly.

When you receive the information, along with photocopies for your files, read and study what the law says. To most people it will be somewhat difficult the first time because laws are in legalese, i.e., lawyer double-talk. Pick them up again in a day or so and reread them, and more of it will make sense to you. After doing this a few times, you will start to have a better idea as to what the law says about the licensing of PIs in your state. Now, after doing all of this, let me just say that what the law says and means and the way things are done where you live may not always be the same.

Strange as it may seem, just because the law says this is the way it is supposed to be done doesn't always make it so.

The next step is to talk to the government agency that is responsible for licensing in your state or locale, if possible. The law that governs the licensing of PIs should specify where to apply for a license. You can also call your state capital and ask the information office whether there is a state licensing board. If there is a specific board designated for PIs, the information office should be able to put you in touch with someone who could help you. If there is no state agency that oversees private investigators, check with your local county and city governments. Your local police or sheriff department could be another source for this information.

If you have a local city agency that you can call or visit, do so. If you are a young person, I suggest that you call and try to set up an appointment with the person in that office who has the most knowledge about licensing. If you show genuine respect and a true interest in learning this, that person will likely try to give you some time and answer most of your questions. Anyone can try this, although the staff will probably be a little less tolerant of such legal inquiries from an older person. They may suggest that you seek counsel of an attorney because it is not their job to provide that kind of legal information. But don't let this discourage you from trying. There are a lot of people in these agencies just waiting to be helpful, although there are always a few who are not.

The next step is to talk to someone who has really been there—as in worked as a private detective. Go talk to a licensed PI. I saved this for last in this chapter because to get the PI to talk to you may require showing him/her that you have started your research and that you are serious about learning more about how to become a PI. At the outset, you want to make it clear to the PI that you are not asking for a job but seeking information about PIs. Express your interest in the profession and explain that you are a student who is trying to learn more about the legal licensing of PIs and you are doing an assignment in a self-study program.

You may have to call or visit a number of PIs. Some may be just too busy at the time to help you. If one is too busy, call or visit the next one on your list. Again, as when talking to the person at the licensing agency, you must show that you are sincerely interested in learning what it takes to become a PI. You may want to show that you have already done some research and talked to others in this quest for some very specific information. Make it clear that this is something important to you and not just a passing interest. If necessary, make an appointment for a time that is most convenient for him or her and make sure that you are on time. Go prepared with a list of questions and be ready to take notes. Ask specific questions as they relate to your state and see if you can get examples, if appropriate. Things you might consider asking include the following: Do I need an attorney to apply? Are there any hidden fees involved in getting a license? How long does it take? What kind of experience or education is required? Is age a factor? What would prevent someone from being licensed? Have the laws changed much over the years, and do you see any changes forthcoming? These should help get you started.

To make a list of PIs, check the telephone book to see if there are any already in your area. You may also be able to get the names and addresses of local PIs from the licensing government agency. This information should be public record and readily available. (So before you leave the licensing agency, remember to request a copy of all PIs in your area.) You may be surprised to learn how many licensed PIs there are in your area. Many never advertise in the yellow pages.

In your search for a PI to talk to, see if you can find out who has been around the longest, because his or her experience and knowledge could obviously prove very helpful to you. Next, check to find out which ones have been licensed most recently and seek them out for their knowledge of the most recent licensing procedures. If possible, talk to several to get an overview of what is required to become a PI. You may be surprised to find that two PIs from the same state, if they work in different cities or counties, will tell you different things about the way one gets licensed.

Be prepared with your questions. Once you find one who is willing and has the time to talk, don't lose him by not being ready. When you are done visiting, either by telephone or in person, ask if you may contact him or her again if you have further questions. If you are at an office, be sure to get a business card. If you are speaking on the telephone, make sure you have his or her full address before hanging up. If there are no PIs for you to visit locally, you may have to do some traveling or make a number of long distance telephone calls. Keep track of those with whom you did and did not speak.

And now for one of the most important parts of your training: send the people you speak with a thank-you for their time. Let me repeat that—*send them a thank-you for their time*. This is one of the most important things you can do. Take my word for it, they will appreciate it. Today, in too many cases, this is not done. Etiquette is a thing of the past. Doing this shows people that you appreciate the time and the efforts they put forth to help you.

ASSIGNMENT

1. What state laws (if any) apply to PIs in your state? (title, section, subsection)

_____

_____

_____

_____

2. What local laws (if any) apply to PIs in your locale? (title, section, subsection)

_____

_____

_____

_____

_____

3. What agency of the state or local government governs the licensing of PIs in your state?

_____

_____

_____

_____

_____

4. Who is the closest PI with whom you could visit and consult?

_____

_____

_____

_____

_____

5. What outside reading have you done that would help you become a better PI?

_____

_____

_____

_____

_____

CHAPTER THREE

GET READY

The most important thing you can do to prepare for a career in private investigation is to *get an education*. Yes, that means staying in school. It means reading things that may seem boring at the time. You will have to give up something for this education. Sometimes that may mean you can't attend a party on a Saturday night because you're working to pay for your education. You may have to do an internship without pay just to work with others who are already established in the field. Yes, this education will have a price, and you must be willing to pay it. But only with this education will you be able to become a private detective others will want to hire.

Think of it this way: if you needed an operation, would you go to a doctor who was only second rate and operated that way? As private detectives, we must prepare ourselves the same way any professional does. Our education may be more unconventional than that of doctors or other professionals, but we still must get it. Depending on the type of work you do or choose to specialize in as a private investigator, you may find yourself at night school studying law to help you in courtroom preparation or in another state attending seminars on blood spattering to assist you in murder investigations. Whatever the training, it will require your time and probably your money.

THE IMPORTANCE OF A HIGH SCHOOL DIPLOMA

As a young person, you may think getting an education to become a PI seems unnecessary. You've seen on TV and in the movies that all we ever do is have car chases and shootouts and get into a lot of fights. These scenarios are definitely the exceptions. In reality, you will find that you will exercise your brain more than anything else you do. Most of the investigators I know have obtained a college education, and often they've done postgraduate work or have continued to attend seminars in order to better themselves. They all read trade magazines that relate to the type of investigations they do.

Let yourself be entertained with the TV and movie detectives, but don't let these perceptions of private detectives control your ambitions. Sometimes you can "fly by the seat of your pants," but most of the time you must have some real intelligence and know what you're doing. Most modern detective agencies hire people who are articulate, intelligent, and well trained in their area of investigation, and they pay them accordingly. There are still some private detectives who believe all you need to do is talk loud, drink hard, and lie a little to get the job done. Such detectives may always be around, but very few, if any, are really successful or last very long. It is the person who prepares mentally and maintains a professional attitude who will become the consummate investigator.

As a licensed private detective, I have numerous people come to me wanting to become PIs. When I have the time, I try to learn a little about them. I usually ask that they send me a résumé. More times than not, they never do. If I do get a résumé, I look it over and see if the individual shows any ambition. On occasion I have gotten résumés from people who have not yet finished high school. A friend asked me to talk to someone he knew who wanted to be a PI. I met the young man at my office. He brought his résumé with him. Though he was a nice young man who was working in another job at a low management level, he had not graduated from high school. He explained to me that he was going to get his GED. I told him that although I did not need any extra help at that time, I might in the future, and I would consider him after he earned his GED. At that time, he promised to get his GED in the very near future. Several months later I talked to him again, and he told me he was no further along in getting his GED than he was earlier. At that moment, I decided what he really meant was that he was not serious about becoming a PI. It is very doubtful that I would ever consider him for employment with my agency. What he probably did not realize was that, as a prospective employer, not only do I consider the high school education important, but I look for people who will continue to educate themselves. He was not even willing to do just enough to get by.

COLLEGE

A high school education is just the beginning. I would be the first to recommend a good liberal arts education to anyone who is considering this work. But this is not the only option to the aspiring PI. Not everyone is cut out for a conventional college education right after high school. You might be more suited to enter the workplace and put aside some money for when you do decide to go back to school. At the same time, you could do some research on your own.

If you are not ready to enter college full time, consider going part time. One class at a time, or even a night class, can help you continue your education. You could work full time and still acquire an education. Many community colleges give you an opportunity to continue your education with a varying schedule and at a price most people can afford. More and more colleges are offering police courses at off-campus locations and at times that are convenient for everyone. If you are still in high school, talk to your guidance counselor about what colleges offer the type of course or curriculum you are looking for. If you are out of school, check out your local library and see if it has catalogs from the colleges in your area. More and more private schools and colleges have sites on the Internet, via the World Wide Web. Many schools and public libraries have access to the Internet and can offer assistance if you don't know how or where to start.

SPECIALIZED TRAINING AND SEMINARS

On a personal note, I must tell you something I did more than 20 years ago. After graduating from high school, I started attending a local community college the following fall. I was majoring in police science at the time. About a month into the semester I learned from a friend that some local police officers were taking a continuous training course that met two evenings a week at my old high school. After checking it out, I found out that it was a vehicle code course being taught by the state police. I approached the instructor, explaining I was a college student majoring in police science and that I was wondering if I could sit in on their training sessions. Though I was not an official student in the class, I was permitted to attend for the next five weeks. The point here is that if you look for opportunities, you will probably find them. If you ask enough times, some doors will begin to open for you.

MILITARY

You may want to consider the military. Nowhere else will you have the opportunity to learn skills and get the responsibility that goes with them. The price you pay will be that not only will you learn to discipline yourself, but you will live that discipline from day one. The military will teach you its way of doing things, which will be helpful to a PI but that will also help you in any job you may do as well as in your personal life. There is a catch, though. You must want to learn these things. Like anything you do, going into the military can be either time wasted or a school that serves as the basis for what you do the rest of your life. This is not to say that you will enjoy everything you do in the service. Many things you do will make no sense to you at the time. You may even find that at times you completely disagree with your order. You may also think you know how to do something better or the right way, and you will not be able to do anything about it. But consider it the price you must pay to get the education you receive. Last, the military can give you that break you may need between high school and college, as well as allowing you to earn benefits to pay your way through college.

SELF-STUDY

Going to college or into the military isn't the only way—or necessarily even the best way—to get an education. Books afford all of us the opportunity to improve ourselves. Building your own library is important. But the books must be read to be helpful. Investing in books is one of the wisest things you can do to prepare yourself. I always tell people that if you get just one piece of information from a book, it is probably worth the price of the book.

Open almost any magazine, and if it has a classified section you'll probably find at least one ad for courses on how to become a PI. I have observed a number of these and found that they are good as far as they go. Most are generic and provide some information in the different areas of investigation. If you choose to take one of these courses, I suggest that you follow up on your own on each of the subjects it covers. For example, you may be required to read about how to do surveillance. Don't just rely on what was in the course. Go out and find several other books on the subject. Next, research where you might have to use these techniques. Consider what kind of cases might require you to do these things. Next, research these types of cases and find out what else you might have to know to do them better. What skills might you have to develop or refine to do the complete job? Will you need special equipment for these types of cases?

TRADE SCHOOLS

In the last decade there has been a rise in private trade schools. These schools are usually registered or licensed within the state where they operate. This in itself, though, does not mean that the state endorses or places any value on their programs or their certificates of graduation. It just means that they are licensed to operate a private school and make money by doing just that.

Many of these schools do provide a good education in different kinds of programs and prepare their students to some degree to do the job for which they are training. Unfortunately, though, many just get students to obligate themselves with student loans, usually through some government guarantee program, and then provide little, if any, real education. If you do find one of these schools that provides training that you think would assist you in your venture, do some investigating before enrolling. Ask them how they assist with placement of their graduates. Ask for a list showing where former students have been placed, whether they are still there, and what their starting pay was. Call former students and confirm what you were told.

As with any type of training, do not be pressured into something of which you are unsure. Very few things require that you make a decision on a moment's notice, and no reputable school should pressure you to do so. Look at all of your options and then make a decision based on what you have learned about each of the different training programs you've researched.

• • • • •

After saying all this about being careful, let me also say that this should not prevent you from taking action to become a PI. You must take action to bring about results. It is still up to you to take the first step. Do your best to make the right decision, and when in doubt, realize that sometimes you will still have to do something you are not sure of. You may make mistakes, but learn from them so you'll make a better decision the next time.

Experience is one of the best educators, but a foundation in formal education is invaluable. What you learn can never be taken from you. It may seem unlikely now, but someday you will be amazed by how something you learned a long time ago suddenly helps you in a way you never would have imagined. Here's something to think about: the mind is never full. You will always have room for more information. In reality, scientists have not been able to accurately measure how much of our minds we really use. Some suggest we only use about 10 percent of it. Others say that the capability of the mind is infinite. But it is up to us to use it and control what we put into it.

To conclude this chapter, let me just say that opportunities are out there for everyone to learn, but you have to take advantage of them. No one else is going to do it for you. The PI profession is one that does not need undermotivated or uneducated people pursuing it.

ASSIGNMENTS

1. On a separate piece of paper, list all of the education you have had. List all schools, colleges, trade schools, and correspondence schools you have attended, as well as any in-house training or other kind of training you may have had. When finished, put this in a file folder called "My Résumé."

2. On a separate piece of paper, list all of the jobs you may have had or done. Highlight any work that would include experience in security, investigation, law

enforcement, or safety. When finished, put this in the file folder called "My Résumé."

3. In the back of most men's magazines are advertisements for mail order private detective training. Request information from no less than three. When it arrives, read it completely. Look for what is good and not so good about each. Make notes and put all of this in a separate file folder with the school or course name on it.

4. Locate the closest college or trade school that offers courses in the area of police science, investigation, or security. When you get this information, put it in a file folder with the school/college name on it.

CHAPTER FOUR

YOUR PRIVATE OFFICE

Whether you are a young person still in school or someone older planning to work your way into becoming a private detective, your own private office area can be one of your most valuable tools. You may not want to hear this, but this is probably where you will spend a good bit of your time, both in training to become a PI and when you are one. Many times the office is where the cases start and where it is all put together. It is where you learn, research, communicate, and express yourself. Clients contact you through your office, and you will do much of your work for them in your office. It is where you will read and write reports. It is where your business day usually begins and ends. Make your private office a pleasant, effective place to work.

When I say private office, I am talking about a separate area that is set aside specifically for you to perform your duties as a PI. For the young person, it might have to be your bedroom, but you should still try to designate it as a distinct part of your room. If you are fortunate to have a spare room, whether it is in the basement, the attic, or even the garage, use it. If you have your own place, find a space where you can work comfortably as floor space permits. Since you are just starting out, you may not need to rent office space apart from where you live at this point. The purpose here is to develop some office skills (which you will need), some more self-discipline, and organization.

YOUR DESK

Your office should start with a desk. It doesn't have to be fancy, but it would be better to have one too large than too small. Your desk is the focus of your office space. Even if you do not have much room for your private office, your desk should get primary consideration in apportioning room space before adding any other equipment or furniture. I have seen desks ranging from a pair of two-drawer file cabinets with the smooth side of a finished door placed on top of them, to folding tables, to the top-of-the-line executive desk. At first it will not really matter what it looks like as long as you can work on it. If you have a little money available, I suggest checking out office furniture/supply stores for a used desk that is comfortable for you. Also, check the classified ads in your local newspaper and don't forget to check the neighborhood-shopper newspaper for ads for used desks. Of course, if you just inherited some money from your Aunt Edna and can afford to spend some real money, go first class and get one that will last a lifetime and at the same time show timeless style and elegance. (This touches on what I will discuss later in the chapter on your image.)

A desk to consider if space is limited is a secretary's desk—one with a cabinet and a shelf that pulls out and holds a typewriter. One of the drawers should be designed to hold file folders. In obtaining a desk like this you eliminate the need for a full-size file cabinet and typewriter stand. Later, if you need to, you can get these.

A FILE CABINET

If your desk does not have a file drawer in it, consider purchasing a file cabinet. When you finally get the room and/or the money for one, you will be faced with several options, dealing mostly with size. The drawers can be either legal or letter size. You can get two-drawer, four-drawer, or even five-drawer cabinets. Even the length of the drawers will vary. The better cabinets will have a quality roller on the drawers, whereas others will just slide metal on metal. They can come with simple locks on each drawer or a single lock that locks the entire cabinet. You can even add high-security bar locks later, if necessary, which I do recommend.

The first thing you should decide on is file size—legal or letter size. Legal-size file folders generally hold papers that are up to 8 1/2 by 14 inches. Letter-size file folders are designed to hold papers up to the standard 8 1/2-by-11-inch size. What does it really matter? As you progress with this training process, you will probably obtain papers in both sizes. Tablets come in both legal and letter size. Why are there two sizes, anyway? Why is there always someone out there trying to make things harder than they should be? Why ask? Because that's why you are who you are. You're probably just nosy like me. Well, when lawyers wrote things up a long time ago, they needed a little more space to add their seal at the bottom of the paper. Hence, we have the longer legal paper. In researching this little phenomenon, I learned recently that many states are now using standard-size paper and eliminating the legal size. It seems that even though legal-size paper may be the standard for the judicial world, it is not for the rest of us. More of the government's legal paperwork is being sized to match that of the rest of the world. With modern printing processes, computers, and photocopiers, it's just easier now to standardize the size of forms and documents. For now, the most practical solution may be to choose a file cabinet that will accommodate both types of file folders.

Next to consider is the number of drawers you want in one cabinet. Will you have room for whatever you get? I suggest that if you have the room and the money, buy the four- or five-drawer cabinet. You will find that even though you may not fill all the drawers right away with your PI files, it will be ideal for your personal files and some of your extra office supplies. If you don't have the room, go with the two-drawer size, but move up to a larger one when you can. You'll be glad you did.

The next consideration when looking for a file cabinet is the way the drawers move in the cabinet. Now, at this point you may be thinking that this investigator may have sniffed a little too much gun oil, but stay with me. You're probably saying to yourself that drawers only go in two directions—in and out. True, but how well they go in and out will make a big difference in the long run.

For the first few years, you will be the only person opening and closing these drawers. You will soon discover that some move more easily and smoothly than others. Cheaply made file cabinets slide in and out, bare metal on bare metal. In my opinion, these are nothing but trouble. Not only are these hard to open and close, but they are usually made out of very thin metal. If you try setting anything on top of them, they will warp and become almost impossible to open and close. Chances are, too, that if you brush up against this type of cabinet, it will probably snag your clothes. Often the drawers have sharp corners, and even if the drawer is closed, it is a good bet that one of the corners is sticking out just enough to hook you. Ladies, these cabinets just eat up pantyhose.

What you want to look for are those great little things called roller-bearings or ball-bearings; usually the more of these, the better. Open a drawer and look along the side of it. Some will have rollers on the side of the drawer itself. Others will have a bar that comes out along with the drawer but only half as far as the drawer itself. These bars will have roller- or ball-bearings on them. This second type is better than the first, because, again, the more the better. If you pull the drawer out all the way, extended completely and then lift on the front of the drawer, it will release itself from the cabinet. This way you can take a closer look as to how well the cabinet is made. Before you buy one, look at a number of them and find out how a good one looks and feels and then make your decision.

Another thing to look for is whether the cabinet comes with a lock or if one can be installed easily. The nature of your work requires that you keep things locked up. This is not to say that you can stop someone from destroying a file cabinet and taking everything out of it, but it will keep nosy people out of files and other places where they don't belong. If the cabinet does not have a lock or the internal mechanism for one but has sufficient strength to serve your purposes, consider installing a bar lock. You can get one from a local locksmith. By the way, if you haven't made friends with one of these guys by now, this would be a good time. You can both benefit from each other's clients.

A minor thing to think about here is manila file folders. Again, there are letter and legal sizes; you'll probably want to have both. Next look at the tabs at the top. Some folders come with the tabs all in the same place. All of my file folders have tabs that are on the right-hand side. That way I can look straight back through the drawer and find what I am looking for. You can get folders with all of the tabs on the left-hand side too. Finally, you can get file folders that have tabs that are placed in three to five different positions across the top. Buy a box and try one type for awhile. If you don't like one type, switch before you get too many files. You can always use the former type of file folders for reports you give to clients. It's not necessary when you first start out, but you can also get special colored labels for the tabs to help you keep things in order and avoid misfiling things. You will better understand this someday when you are asked to look over an old file and discover that it's not where it belongs. Color-coded tabs will help you detect misfiled folders more easily by limiting their possible locations to a very small area. Your local office supply store can advise you further as to what's available.

TELEPHONE

There is not really much to say here except that you will need a telephone. For a young person, a private line may not be possible. Respect for the family telephone and those who pay for it must be upheld. For the older person who is setting up an office, the private line is a must. Clients must have a way of getting in touch with you. Your telephone is your lifeline to information. It is a tool that can and will make money for you. Your telephone line can also be used for other electronic tools, such as a fax machine and computer modem.

The basic telephone with good tonal qualities is your first concern. You have to sound good on the phone. In many cases, a telephone conversation will make a first impression for you. Make sure it is the best-sounding telephone possible. Don't get a phone that sounds like you're calling from inside a tunnel or that pops and crackles when you are talking to someone. You must be heard clearly and be understood at all times when you are communicating, whether it is with a client, source, or witness.

Next, since your telephone is a tool you will probably be using quite a bit, get one that is comfortable to use. One that looks like your favorite car or has some abstract modern art design will probably get to be quite a pain after awhile. The new buzz word is ergonomic design. Try holding your phone to your ear with your shoulder for awhile. A good telephone will rest easily and remain more comfortable much longer. Pads for standard handsets are available, again from your office supply store.

An even better option is using a headset. This is one of those things you used to see telephone operators using. Now they are available for everyone. They free up your hands for writing, opening books and file drawers, and working while you are on the phone. They are being used more by professionals every day. And now their prices have dropped so just about anyone can purchase one. If you find that you are on the telephone a lot, get one. Speaker phones were popular for a while, but they just did not have the right sound and were difficult to use. Trust me—for hands-free operation, forget the speaker phone and get a headset.

Just about everywhere in the United States you can get Touch Tone service. Get it and use it. Naturally, you will need a Touch Tone telephone. If your telephone has a speed dialer, consider it a bonus. Phone systems that allow you to program in one-number dialing for frequently called numbers are also a plus. Cordless phones give you free range to work away from your desk and move around your office. But a better accessory for your telephone would be your personal phone file. Whether it be a Rolodex, a computer phone book, or the standard personal address book with telephone numbers, make sure you keep it up to date and it will be a valuable tool.

ANSWERING MACHINE

Unless you can hire a personal secretary, bribe a family member, pay for an answering service, or avoid ever leaving your office, you will need an answering machine. Since you will be out of the office often, you need to give everyone who calls an opportunity to leave you a message or contact you by some other means. When I am not available to take calls, the message on my answering machine directs clients to leave a message and tells them how to contact me on my beeper.

As far as answering machines go, my best suggestion is to purchase a name brand that is either a newer digital model or has dual tapes for incoming and outgoing messages. Most single-tape machines can be confusing to the caller if he or she happens to be the third or fourth caller. When there are several messages on the machine, many times there will be a long wait between the outgoing message and the point at which the caller is supposed to leave a message. Also, as with some cheaper telephone models, some machines sound bad. Remember, the message you leave and the quality of its sound may be the first impression of you that callers get. Don't let it be the only time they get to hear your voice.

YOUR STATIONERY

What do you currently write your letters on? If you have stationery, pick up a piece of it. How does it look? Is the letterhead printed or do you have to type it on? If you have a computer, does it put your letterhead on the paper?

Now I'm going to tell you something you probably will not want to hear. Even if you think your stationery looks great, it probably does not. The best analogy is that if what you have now is the "two-for-the-price-of-one polyester leisure suit of stationery," you should switch to the stationery that is the equivalent of the thousand-dollar Brooks Brothers three-piece suit.

This is one area in which you should spend money—and spend it right the first time. If you start dealing with those who have considerably more money than yourself, they will recognize quality paper. They usually handle it everyday. Cheap paper leaves a cheap impression. Good, expensive paper tells people that you appreciate quality and that you are probably worth the money you command. (Please note, though, that any and all impressions can be shattered with poor quality, inappropriate behavior, and lack of respect for the people with whom you are dealing. First impressions open doors, so once you're in, don't do things to get yourself thrown out.)

A PI's letterhead should look as professional as the professional he wants to work for. In most cases, it should be clean looking and uncluttered. The envelope should either match exactly or be white printed with a single color of ink. If possible, your business card should match your letterhead; again, a single color of ink on bright white card stock. Cute images may be okay for some other business, but most of the time they do little to promote you as a professional.

Now, having said all of that, I will say that there are always exceptions. I will be the first to say that if you have found something that works for you and does an outstanding job of bringing in the clients you want to work for, all the better. Nothing is carved in stone, and new ideas should always be considered. However, based on my own experience, I would definitely go with the heavy, white, expensive, watermarked bond paper with matching envelopes. I had to learn the hard way.

As strange as it may seem, I have three different business cards that I use for different things. The first is printed with my name, title, and telephone number. It is for giving to people whom I interview and to whom I do not find it necessary to offer my address. The second card is shaped like a rotary file card with name, title, address, and telephone number. This one matches my letterhead in color and ink. The third is a professional-looking card, black on white, with all the information. This is for when I first meet a client or attorney and I want to make a professional impression.

A printer can show you lots of different kinds of paper, layouts, and designs and put them all together for you. I would suggest that you be careful and not let anyone's artistic urges take control of the situation. This is one time where simple is good. Most printers can print the items for you or show you items from a catalog that they send out to be completed. Look at the examples that they have printed before. Look at their catalog of items that they farm out to larger specialized companies. Let them show you different types of papers, sizes (stick with standard sizes), and weights. Font, or the typeface, should be kept simple yet dignified. If you print something in the old English style of lettering, people may be asking you what the address or telephone number is or, worse yet, what your name is because they can't read it. If you find it necessary to list all of the things you do or want to list other information, consider putting it on the back. Have this as a second card, but still have the elegant, professional card to make the best first impressions.

A COMPUTER

At first, I was going to write that a computer could be an option for the young apprentice, someone opening a new office, or even the old pro. But now, more than ever, it is not an option but rather one of the most important pieces of equipment you should have. Those who do not have and use a computer today are truly holding themselves back personally and financially. They are also doing a disservice to their clients by not using this labor- and cost-saving device. For these reasons, the personal computer (PC) is no longer an option but a necessary tool of the trade.

As I write this, the prices of PCs are dropping like bad clichés in an old detective novel. Trust me, if you really want to do this work, forget buying the new BMW for a while and get a good PC. Don't worry about prices; they are always coming down, and what you pay for today will probably be cheaper tomorrow. But don't wait—you will wait yourself out of work.

Why do you need a computer? Again, trust me. If you plan on doing any reports, you'll want a computer. Think back to the last time you typed a report on a typewriter. If you're still in school now, you may never have and probably will never have to. If you're a little older, like me, just try typing a two-page, single-spaced report with no mistakes. Now go back and add two lines that you forgot. It's no fun, is it? Hence, one of the main reasons for having a computer—with a good printer—is to use it as a word processor. Sure, word processors are cheaper than computers, but word processing is all they can do.

Next, a computer can do your bookkeeping for you if you install an accounting program. This is something that you will want done correctly, right from the beginning. You can create data bases for your cases and retrieve information on them almost instantly. With a computer, you have your own ready-made forms. I say this because a lot of PIs who are just starting out like to have forms for just about everything. They think it makes their paperwork easier. Forms do help to organize information, but at the same time, they create a lot of unnecessary paper to file.

With telephone lines, your computer can send and receive

faxes and e-mail and communicate with on-line services such as CompuServe, America Online, and Delphi. Each of these offers resources at your fingertips. Information that you would not otherwise have readily accessible can now be obtained quickly and easily. This information will not include private or classified files, but it does comprise things that might take you days to find if you had to obtain it yourself or send for it by other means. You can even meet other private detectives and aspiring PIs on-line. You can trade tips or learn new techniques or sources of important information. Last but not least, the computer can connect you to the Internet. This information superhighway will be a major part of almost everyone's lives in the very near future.

Again, *trust me*—a computer is very necessary for your business or almost any profession today. Within the limited space of just this book, I can't go into all the reasons why you should have a computer and how it will help you. It will require further investigation on your part on what is right for you, what you can afford to start with, and the type of software most suited to your needs. Yes, you'll need software, too. Shop, ask questions of those who know, learn, and then get one that is right for you.

A TYPEWRITER

A *typewriter*? Here I just spent a lot of time on why you need a computer, and now I'm telling you to get a typewriter. Yes, you need a typewriter. Have you ever tried to fill out a form on a computer? It can be done, but only if the form is already programmed into your computer. This can be done fairly easily if you have a scanner, but if not, it is somewhat difficult to do.

The fact is, sometimes it is just quicker and easier to do something on a typewriter. Also, your computer may be tied up with something else just when you have to type up only one envelope and mail it before the postman comes. Besides, you can pick up a decent one for under a hundred dollars, and you will still be using it long after your computer is out-dated by new technology in several years.

The basic thing to look for in a decent typewriter is the quality of the type. The letters must be sharp and line up even-ly. A short while back, dot matrix models were available. Most were designed to be portable and somewhat inexpensive. They may have been acceptable for a term paper, but not in the pro-fessional world. Stay away from them. Electric is usually preferable to manual. Make sure you can still get ribbons for the model you choose and at a reasonable price. A typewriter with interchangeable wheels or typefaces is also good. The ability to change them when they get old looking or are not as sharp as they should be keeps your correspondence looking professional. Whether new or used, typewriters are out there at very reasonable prices.

By the way, if you do not know how to type or use a key-board, you had best start learning now. The seek-and-destroy or hunt-and-peck method of typing was okay for the occa-sional high school report, but not in the new computer age. Learn keying now, no matter what your age. It will speed up your work dramatically, which will make you more efficient and give you an edge over your competition.

DICTATION EQUIPMENT

You'll be glad to hear that this equipment is an option. To start, a hand-held microcassette recorder is nice to have for field notes. IMPORTANT NOTE: *Don't use it for illegal recording of conversations.* You can use a microrecorder to dictate notes, letters, and reports that can be transcribed later. Desktop recorders are also available with all kinds of features, most of which you wouldn't need for a while. A secretary listens to the cassette using a playback machine controlled by a foot switch, which frees the hands up for typing the dictation. Again, an elaborate dictation system is optional and should only be pur-chased when you reach the point where you can justify hiring someone to do the secretarial work for you. If this is something you can use, again, shop around. These devices are available at office supply, department, and numerous other types of stores. There are also several companies that specialize in brand-name equipment such as Dictaphone and Lanier. Their equipment will cost more up front, but the quality and technical support will make up for the price in the long run. If you have enough business to justify purchasing this equipment, get the best you can afford. It really pays off in the long run.

YELLOW-RULED TABLETS

Get letter-size, good-quality yellow tablets for your general everyday notes. Reporter-type notebooks and steno tablets are okay for some people in the field, but I have found that most of the time they just aren't necessary. Get tablets with paper that is big enough to write on. Buy them in bulk and use them. Enough said.

DESK STUFF

Invest in a good stapler and good staples. Cheap ones will just make you angry. Paper clips, everyday pens, rubber bands, and tape should be bought in bulk. You'll save money, and you'll always have them when you need them. Again, invest in quality, because you will be glad you did in the long run. Strong, shiny paper clips will make a better impression than cheap, weak ones. Leaky pens can ruin your day. Tape that doesn't come off the roll doesn't do anybody any good. And cheap rubber bands break down and lose their elasticity when they get old. These items don't cost that much, and paying just a little more will eliminate some unnecessary headaches.

One final point—when you buy a desk, chair, or any other item for your office, make sure it reflects the image you want to convey to clients.

ASSIGNMENTS

1. Measure the area that you want to use as office space. Next, on a piece of paper, draw a diagram of where furniture and equipment (e.g., desk, chair, typing and/or computer table, file cabinet) would be placed. Work with your diagram to see if all of the available space is being used to its full potential.

2. Visit office supply stores and request their catalogs. Most will give you a standardized catalog of what they have and can order for you. Ask if they can discount the prices listed. Also, ask to be put on their mailing list so that you will be informed about upcoming sales. Last, ask whether they sell used furniture and equipment.

3. If you don't know about computers, learn. Meet and get to know someone who can teach you about them. With this person's help, make a wish list of what kind of computer you should get, as well as the type of basic software to go with it.

4. Visit a printer and get samples of papers used for stationery. Next, visit several attorneys and ask for samples of their stationery. Let them know what you are doing so they don't think you are too strange. They will probably want to void samples so that you cannot use them personally. Compare the quality and see which one makes the best impression on you.

5. Start putting things in file folders. Do this even if you do not have a file cabinet. Use a storage box to hold them temporarily.

6. Picture an office that greatly impressed you. Make a list of the reasons you were so impressed.

CHAPTER FIVE

FIELD EQUIPMENT

As a private detective, you will find that you will need certain equipment with you while doing an investigation. Not every investigator needs the same equipment for field work, but there are some basic requirements that most will find essential. In this chapter I will discuss those that I have found to be the most useful. By now, you should know that whenever possible, I try to save myself and you, the reader, some money. Used equipment or good-quality, no-name brands are available for most of the things I will tell you about.

BINOCULARS

If you do any kind of investigation out in the field, a good pair of binoculars should be at the top of your list of equipment. Until you know about all of the expensive brands out there to spend megabucks on, start looking first within your own family. Binoculars are one of those things somebody in the family, at some point, was sure he or she needed. That someone probably saw a good pair on sale and bought them. After the binoculars were played with for a short time, they ended up in the hall closet, forgotten. Now, being a detective in training, you can check out your family—including aunts, uncles, in-laws, and anyone else willing to claim to be part of the family—and let them all know you are looking for a good set. Maybe you'll get a good deal.

If you must purchase a pair, as with most things, a good

rule of thumb is never to buy the cheapest or the most expensive. Most companies have several models of whatever product they sell. There will be the top of the line with all the buttons, whistles, and bells. There will also be the bottom of the line with the minimum features. Many times these low-end items are totally inadequate for anyone who will want to use them seriously. The company makes a bare-bones product and just puts its name on it to get a sale. Name recognition goes a long way in selling products. But be forewarned—just because a product has a popular name on it does not make it superior to another that is more generic. Often, better-quality off-brand equipment with more features costs the same or less than a brand-name model with fewer or inferior features.

Realistically, there are many factors other than price to consider when buying equipment like binoculars. Guarantees, service, and reliability should also be taken into consideration. But the price is probably the most important consideration for the beginning detective.

When you pick up a pair of binoculars, you will see a set of numbers stamped or printed near the eyepieces. They will look like a multiplication problem you might have had back in elementary school—something like 7 X 35, which is common on many binoculars. These numbers will tell you two things about the binoculars you have in your hands: the first nuber refers to their power of magnification, and the second number refers to the diameter of the lens. Most people might believe the first number is important and simply dismiss the second. In reality, both are equally important. Having a powerful pair of binoculars is essential, but if they are too dim to see out of, they are useless. This is where the second number comes in. If the lens is too small for the size and magnification of the binoculars, you will have poor visibility in low-light situations.

There are all sizes of binoculars, from small, palm-sized models to large, tripod-mounted units. There are advantages and disadvantages to all. Binoculars that have a high magnification will give a shakier image if you do not hold them perfectly still. Conversely, if your binoculars are not powerful enough, you will not be able to "bring in" what you are trying to see.

My favorite binoculars that I carry in my vehicle are no-name-brand 7 X 50s. The power is good, and with the 50mm front lens I can see very well, even in low-light situations. Short of using infrared scopes and night vision equipment, this size of binoculars is hard to beat. In fact, if you were to use one of the light-amplifying or infrared devices, your detail would be lost and would have to be made up with a more powerful magnification. With basic optical magnification, things are much clearer, with finer details.

My 7 X 50s are good for use in my vehicle, but I would not like to carry them around my neck all day because they are a little heavy. When I have to walk around, I have a smaller 7 X 35 set. Instead of heavy metal tubes, this pair is made of a lighter metal with a rubber coating. They make me look more like someone who is sightseeing, so I don't stand out as much. They also fit into a small camera bag.

Before buying binoculars, shop around and learn about things like multicoated lenses, easy focusing, quality, and all those features that make them more expensive. Camera shops can probably tell you more about the optics and what is good or bad about them. Outdoor adventure shops can tell you more about what holds up under heavy use. Pick them up and look around and see what makes them good. Do they focus easily? Can you hold them steady, or does the image jump around? How far can you see and still read a license plate? These are just some of the things to consider when buying your binoculars. Make the right choice and buy what you can afford. It will be money well spent.

NOTEBOOK

A notebook or a yellow tablet (which is what I usually

use) is essential when you are out in the field. Those with a background in law enforcement are accustomed to using a flip-over notebook. They were taught how to take notes in a somewhat standardized way in a narrow notebook that was easy to carry in a coat or back pocket. As for myself and a growing number of investigators, we prefer a legal pad to take notes. I use my notes primarily to make my reports. In most cases, they are not viewed in the same way that police notes are. (This can vary depending on the state you are in.)

As you progress through your apprenticeship, you will probably have opportunities to review others' notes (i.e., their note-taking style, the type of notebook or pad they use, the number of notes they take, and whether they use shorthand or not). You will probably see many differences between notes. Whatever style of note taking you use, your notes are meant to serve specific functions.

The first is to record precise information about the case and the things you have observed, such as dates and times, addresses, location, and measurements. When you are on a surveillance, you will have to record who did what and when. You will have to note your location at the time of the surveillance. When interviewing people, recording exact quotes of important statements is extremely important.

A second function of note taking, equally important, is that of recording what you have done for your own records. You can take such notes on a legal pad first and later transfer them to a more permanent record, such as a personal log. This log can be handwritten, typed, or logged onto your computer. It is a diary of your professional work. A side note on keeping a log of what you do for your personal records: I know of one investigator who meticulously keeps a log of what he does daily. He has recorded volumes over the course of his career. For him, this has been a career-saver more than once. On at least two occasions, what he was doing on a particular day and time was under question. All he had to do was go back to the appropriate volume, check his own records to refresh his memory of what he was doing then, and then pull documentation of what he was doing at the time from his files. This investigator had kept records of everything. On both occasions, he was able to squelch any doubts about his integrity.

On the other hand, some records you keep could be used against you one day. Even though the people in question may not have done anything wrong, it is not unheard of for people's records, no matter how innocently kept, to be used against them. Words can be taken out of context. What you may have written in jest or tongue-in-cheek may be misinterpreted. Even the truth, accurately recorded, can be used against you. If it is known that you keep such records and you find yourself in a legal confrontation, rest assured that your records will be subpoenaed. You may not be able to keep them out of your opponent's hands.

Having said all of that, let me leave you with some final thoughts on keeping a personal log. If you keep one, understand that you are making a record that someday may be viewed by others. Is what you are doing and writing something you can be proud of? If you were to read this about someone else, would you question his or her integrity? This is more a matter of doing things that you will be proud to put on paper and not doing things that are wrong. Are the actions that you are recording those of an honorable man or woman?

On a more personal note, I remember a motivational speaker saying once that a life worth living is a life worth recording. There are reasons for and against keeping a personal log. It is not easy to sit down regularly and put on paper a diary or log if you have never done it before. Many times you will find yourself missing a day or two, and then a week will have gone by. If you decide to keep a log, commit to doing it regularly. If necessary, set it as a goal. If it is part of your daily goal, soon it will become second nature to you. You will even find yourself looking forward to doing it. Become your own Dr. Watson to your own Mr. Holmes.

A MICROCASSETTE RECORDER

For the person taking notes, a microcassette recorder can be an excellent tool. If you are driving and you need to take detailed notes, dictating them into a recorder allows you to record the information so that you can put it on paper later. There will be times when it will be 10 times more efficient to record the information on tape than to take your eyes off your subject just to write down some details. You will be able to get more information at the time and then later filter it into your report. It is better to get too much info than not enough or to miss an important event just because you were taking notes.

A recorder is also excellent for taking oral statements from witnesses and getting the information you need. You will have an exact record of what was said, which you can transcribe into a written statement later. Obviously, the recorded interview is also valuable in that it not only gives you a record of the information you want, but at the same time carries the weight of being in the person's own voice.

AN IMPORTANT NOTE (read this twice): Depending on the state you live in, the recording of someone's conversation without his or her knowledge and consent can be illegal. In my state we have what is known as all-party consent. This means that all those whose conversation is being recorded must be aware of it. Other states allow one-party consent. That is, only one person has to know that the conversation is being recorded. Learn the law of your state and obey it. I will discuss this further in the "Don'ts" chapter.

If you have a subject who is willing to talk with you, ask if you can record the conversation. If the person says yes, all the better. If he or she says no, accept it and take written notes. If you do have permission to record the conversation, there are some important things you should do. First, you must identify yourself, give the date and time, and identify the person you are interviewing. Next, ask the subject to introduce himself. Ask him if he understands that the conversation is being recorded and if you have his permission to record the interview. If the person has not answered yes to the last two questions, stop. Make what you are doing clear to the subject and start over. Get the subject's permission on tape. You could get a written waiver, but it is much better if you have it on tape. Next, you may want to add a few more statements confirming that the person understands that the conversation is being recorded and that you have his permission to do so. Rephrase it in simple, easy-to-understand language so as not to cause any misunderstanding about what is going on. You can then proceed with your interview. When you come to the end of the conversation, you must end the interview with statements similar to those that opened it. You ask again if the interviewee understands that the conversation has been recorded and confirm that you had his permission to do so. You again identify yourself and the person you have just interviewed. Finally, you give the current date and time and state that the interview is over. The closing statement simply confirms and gives extra weight to the fact that the statement given to you was voluntary and that you had permission to record it.

The opening statements are more important than the closing, because it is important to get permission up front. If the person changes his mind halfway into the interview and says he wants it to end, you at least have permission to record the interview up to that point. It is okay to make a reasonable request to continue, but if the person insists on stopping, you must stop recording the interview. Do not bother trying to get a closing permission statement; just stop the recording.

Another nice thing about having a microcassette recorder is that it is good for dictation. It is one of the main reasons they were developed. If in your office you have transcription equipment, it is a great companion. At times when I have been very busy, I have dictated field reports on microcassette and given it directly to the attorneys I'm working for and let their office transcribe it for me. They get what they need, and

I do not have to spend a lot of time on report writing. I also get a copy typed for my records. Not all attorneys' offices will do this for you, but some may. You only have to ask. You could hint or plant the idea in their minds and let them think they thought of it first.

CASH AND PLASTIC

The following may seem unnecessary to mention, but I feel it is important. When you are going out in the field on a case, the type of case you are working on will require you to have a certain amount of cash, change, and sometimes credit cards handy. Sometimes you will need to have just a little with you, and at other times substantially more. If you are just going out to do some interviews locally, it is unlikely that you are going to need a lot of money—maybe just some money for gas, parking change, and a couple of bucks for lunch. You may find that you did not *need* to spend any money, but you did. On the other hand, if you find yourself on a domestic case and the subject hops a plane, how prepared would you be to travel? If your client authorizes you to do whatever is necessary to get the information and has given you a substantial retainer, you had better be ready with cash, credit cards, and an overnight bag.

In this kind of work your pocket money needs will change daily as the cases do. Each time you go out on a case, you must think ahead to what financial needs you could reasonably expect. If you know your subject is a traveler, you had better be ready to travel too. If you are just doing a local interview, are you ready to buy lunch for the interviewee? Do you have change for a parking meter to park close to your subject, or will you have to beg for it or look for someone to break a bill? Whether you're a man or a woman, you can learn something from the Boy Scout's motto, "Be Prepared."

For major expenses, a credit card is a necessity. If you do any traveling, it is a must. It is almost impossible to book a last-minute flight or rent a car without one. Credit cards allow you to book rooms, eat out, and basically travel without having to carry excessive amounts of cash. With one, if you find yourself out of town and low on cash, many times you will be able to get a cash advance. I would encourage you to get a gold card as soon as you qualify. Even though most of the time there is an extra charge for this, the benefits usually outweigh this cost. Each credit card will have different benefits, and costs can vary greatly. If your credit rating is good, you can shop around for the best deal. Check with your local bank first to see what it has to offer on its basic card and its gold card if it has one. Compare interest rates, grace periods, credit lines, security features, and your liability if it is lost or stolen. On the gold cards, what are the extra features? Is insurance provided if you rent a car, and what are the restrictions, if any? If your card is lost or stolen, how quickly can you get a replacement card? Is it a card that is recognized by most businesses? I have the gold card that requires me to pay that month's charges in full when the bill comes. It has served me well over the years, and I find that it is accepted by almost all of the businesses I visit. For the few exceptions, I have the other two major cards just in case.

BUSINESS CARDS

As I discussed earlier, you should have a business card. As you progress through your apprenticeship, you will probably discover that business cards with your name and title, if used properly, will be an asset you will not want to be without. First of all, a business card is your personal, portable billboard. It helps you advertise who and what you are. Second, it will, in the minds of many, legitimize you as a professional. A great number of people are impressed with the printed word, i.e., if it is printed, it must be so. Third, when you give your card to people you meet in the course of an investigation, it helps them remember you. When you give them your care, they will probably keep it, as it is not likely that they will ever meet a real private detective again. They now know a real PI, and they may be more helpful. If they remember something after you have gone, they can get back to you. If they have a problem someday, they now know who to call—you, the private detective who gave them a business card. I have had people call me after almost 10 years just because I gave them a business card once during the course of an investigation. Your business card is a tool you should always have with you.

CELLULAR PHONE

In the early eighties, cellular phones were only affordable for the rich. Today, they are commonplace. The actual phones are practically given away, provided you subscribe to a particular carrier for a period of time. If you are working as a private investigator, having one is almost a necessity. If used wisely, cellular phones can be very cost-effective. The real cost of a cellular phone comes in the amount of time that you use it—for outgoing as well as incoming calls; if you are not careful you may find yourself getting a phone bill that is delivered in a box instead of an envelope. Whether you have a hand-held or a car phone, they are great tools. I have a cellular car phone that I use as necessary. Only a few select clients have my cellular number. This way I control the amount of time spent on the cellular phone, which helps me control my cost. The bottom line is, the more you find yourself away from your office, the more you need a cellular phone.

PAGER

I also have a digital pager so that people can contact me when I'm out of the office and I can get back to them as my time permits. I give my pager number out freely, because it is the best way to get a hold of me. It has a greater range than my cellular phone and costs the same whether I am paged once or a thousand times in a month.

A note about pagers: someday they may become obsolete, but for now, they are still good to have around. They have all kinds of features and now come in various colors, so they can go with any fashion-minded investigator's wardrobe! The one feature that I do like is the vibrate mode. Many times I will be sitting in court during a trial, yet I still want to receive messages on my pager. By setting it to vibrate, I get a quiet, light vibration on my belt instead of beeping when someone pages me. I can still receive my pages without the judge threatening me with contempt of court for making too much noise.

TELEPHONE BOOK

One piece of field equipment many young investigators fail to keep with them is a telephone book. How well do you think you could work in your office if you didn't have a phone book there? The same is true when you are in the field. Okay, maybe it's not practical to be carrying around a monster phone book, but you can keep one in your car. I keep several from my city and the surrounding areas in my van. The main local phone book behind my captain's chair is coverless and worn and torn from constant use. Like my gold card, I never leave home without it.

When you are not in your vehicle, you should still keep a personal phone book close by. Whether it is in your briefcase, datebook, purse, or back pocket, you should have important phone numbers at your fingertips. Update your phone book regularly and keep it close. As you develop sources of information; build special relationships with people, businesses, and government employees; and collect special unlisted numbers, you will never want to be without it. Consider it your mobile Rolodex. Keep it, take care of it, respect it, and protect it.

ASSIGNMENTS

1. Time for a new file in your file cabinet—one for field

equipment. Start gathering information from different stores and suppliers on things like binoculars, micro-cassette recorders, pagers, and cellular phones; different cellular phone carrier companies; and suppliers of business cards. Create a wish list and prioritize it according to those things you feel you need to get first.

2. If cost is important to you, make photocopies of your list and pass it out among your family and friends, letting them know that these are things you are looking to obtain at the best price possible.

CHAPTER SIX

REPORTS

Previously I talked about taking notes and gathering information. Eventually, the time will come when you will have to put on paper what you have observed, discovered, heard, and learned. You will have to write a report. This will cause some of you to break out in a cold sweat. I think back to my days when I was in high school and had to write reports. I used to wish it were one day past the day the report was due and the trauma of writing it were over. Things have changed for me considerably. I no longer wish for the day after a report is due. I have just learned how to write reports that are complete, accurate, and somewhat articulate. And so can you. This does not mean that it will be easy. You will have to work at it.

Early in my journey I did not have any idea how a private detective's report should look, what should be in it, how it should sound when read, or anything else. My police experience did not adequately prepare me for the type of reports I would have to write. I even have a degree in police science, and the police courses I took did nothing to prepare me. Now, having mentioned what did not help me, let me tell you some of the things that did.

First, although my police college courses were no help in writing reports, my college education was. Many college courses require one, if not several, term papers in a semester. When I started college, this was something I truly dreaded. In high school, like many, I got by with the minimum effort in writing reports. I was not prepared for what I would face in college. And, quite frankly, it took me several semesters to learn how to prepare a report properly.

Now it is you who will have to put pen to paper or click the keyboard. In doing this, you will have to collect multiple facts, ideas, and events, and, at times, even your opinions (which will be marked as such) and put them together on paper in the form of a report. This report will also have to be accurate, clear, and complete. Equally important, it must be readable and free of grammatical and spelling errors.

One of the most important tools you have to impress clients is how you communicate. Your words, whether spoken or written, will be used to evaluate you. Hence, it is important that you learn the basics of grammar and rhetoric and sound articulate.

First, it should be obvious that your reports must be either typed or printed from a computer or word processor. If you cannot justify or afford a secretary, you will have to be the one to do this. Like most PIs, I started with using a typewriter and eventually graduated to using a computer. If you must use the typewriter, the most important thing to remember is never be lazy in writing a report just because you hate to type. It seems to take forever to correct any mistakes you make. If you discover the mistake after you've typed the entire page, you either have to correct it as best you can or type the page over. This causes many people to keep their reports very brief, but a report is too brief if it leaves out relevant or important information. Never let the extra work of retyping cause your work to be incomplete.

Now that I have touched on the negative aspects of using a typewriter, let me tell you something good about it. If you are like most people in that you want to keep your typing to a minimum, typing reports will teach you to pick and choose your words more carefully. Being concise is good as long as the report contains all of the necessary information. One page of paper with well chosen words is better than several pages that are vague and/or redundant. If something clarifies or adds to a report, put it in. If it is not necessary or may serve to confuse the reader, leave it out. If it can be said in five words rather than ten, use five.

Now, because most of you will not have a secretary at first, learn to type (or, as most students are taught today, to input information on a computer keyboard). If you are still in school, take the time to learn it now. It will benefit you for the rest of your life. If you are out of school, learn on your own or take a course at night. If you already have a computer, there are a number of very good programs that will teach you to touch type.

A report should be a listing or narrative of the information you have gathered on a particular case. A single case may require you to file many reports or just one. A report can be a log of what happened during a surveillance, a record of what was said during an interview, or a summary of the final results of an investigation. A report will consist of information for a client or attorney to read, understand, and use as he or she sees fit. As you gain experience, you can supplement your reports with memos that offer your opinions and recommendations based on the results of your investigation. These should be separate from the report unless you have reached what is known as "expert status," at which point clients will expect your report to include the opinions you've formed and the conclusions you've drawn as a result of your inquiries, analysis, and investigation.

In high school, when you had to write a report, the teacher often required you to include a title page. Well, guess what—private detectives' reports don't need title pages. What they do need are headers. Okay, you say, what are headers? They are the line of text at the top of every page of your report that summarizes for the reader important information about the report. These can vary in content and style. Usually the report header will include the investigator's name or initials, the company ID number, the clients' or case name, the attorney's name, and the page number with number of total pages for that report. Every detective or agency has a preferred style. Some attorneys may ask you to prepare reports in a special way. Below is an example of the style of header I use most of the time for my reports:

**INTERVIEW REPORT page 1 of 2
ATTORNEY/CASE NAME RJW**

Following the header, you will include other information, such as the subject, date, and time of the report or interview. After this you will begin the body of the report in standard indented paragraph style, single spaced. This gives the report a clean and professional look and makes it easy to read. On interview reports, the first paragraph will include the interviewee's name, address, and telephone number and indicate whether he or she was interviewed in person or by telephone. I also include a reference to the interviewee's apparent disposition (e.g., cooperative, hesitant, upset, etc.) at the time of the interview. This introductory information might look something like this:

Re: John Doe interview
June 1, 1998
4:24 P.M.

On this date and time, this investigator interviewed Mr. John Doe in his home at 123 Main Street, Anytown, PA 12345. His telephone number is 403-456-1234. Mr. Doe spoke openly and freely about his knowledge of the events surrounding the accident on May 1, 1998, at the intersection of Main and State Streets, Anytown, PA.

At the end of the interview report, you will simply type END

OF REPORT or END OF INTERVIEW in all capital letters. The entire brief report may look something like the following example:

INVESTIGATION REPORT page 1 of 1
BAKER/SMITH RJW

Re: Mary Brown, location

July 1, 1998

As requested by attorney Frank Baker, on behalf of client Robert Smith, this investigator conducted a search for missing debtor Mary Brown. Mary Brown had signed a promissory note to Smith and subsequently left the area. As a result of our investigations, as of this date it was learned that the subject now lives at 44 West Second Street, Hometown, PA 12345. Her telephone number is 412-485-9988.

Upon speaking to a neighbor, this investigator also learned that Brown is currently employed at local Main Street Minute Market. Her landlord stated that she resides with another person by the name of James Miller.

END OF REPORT

What I have just shown you is not carved in stone. Your reports need not look just like mine. What is important is that they are complete and presented in a professional manner. Some PIs' reports use forms and are very rigid in their style. Others will be less formal looking yet still complete. As with all things, take the best ideas you are leaning toward and put them together in a format that suits you best. It may not be exactly right the first time, or even the second time, but eventually you will settle on the style that you like the most and that best expresses your work.

ASSIGNMENTS

1. In your local newspaper, find an article concerning a traffic accident. With a pen or highlighter, mark the important facts of the accident. In your own mind, based on the account from the newspaper, create a witness to the accident. Now, again in your mind, interview that person, asking him or her questions and creating appropriate responses. Create a dialogue and take notes. Finally, based on the information in your notes, write an interview report.

2. Again, go back to the local private detective or attorney with whom you have established a relationship. Ask if he or she will evaluate your report. (Naturally, you'll need to explain that even though it is based on a real accident, the report is entirely fictional.)

3. Ask the private detective or attorney if you can review an actual report, but only one of a closed file, i.e., a case file that has been completed or ended for one reason or another but would not create a conflict or problem in the agency or firm.

CHAPTER SEVEN

PHOTOGRAPHY AND VIDEO

Just as your notebook records written information, your cameras record visual information. One word can create thousands of different images for different people. A single picture can replace a thousand words. A photograph is a visual record. It can supplement a report or be its total essence. Because of this, every aspiring private detective needs to learn basic and advanced photography.

In regular photography, you will capture the image of an object, person, or event and preserve it as a still image. In video, you will do the same, except that the viewing medium will show action and any movement of the subject. Many of the same principles will apply to both (e.g., proper framing, holding the camera steady, proper lighting, filtration, and focal lengths of lenses). Each medium has advantages and disadvantages. Overall, still photography offers better resolution and detail. Video has the advantage of showing the detail of something in motion.

STILL PHOTOGRAPHY

Let's start with still photography (from this point on, I will refer to it simply as "photography").

What kind of camera does a PI use? Whatever he has or can get his hands on. Okay, I know you want something a little more specific than that. But in some ways, it's very true.

Almost any camera can be used at one time or another by a PI. In some other cases, though, some very specific photographic equipment is required. If you ever really get serious about photography, you will learn quickly that there are thousands of different makes, models, styles, and formats of cameras, each priced accordingly. The next thing you will learn is that there is a gadget, filter, grip, attachment, holder, article of clothing, flash, idea book, case, tripod, monopod, chestpod, strap, screen, case, quick-release device, hold-fast device, cord, split, mask, hood, viewer, lens shade, or one of more than a thousand features the overly complete photographer will want in a camera. (We will talk about these accessories later.)

Back to what kind of camera you should have. If you have one already, it may be enough to begin with. The novice should have a different camera than the more seasoned photographer/investigator. I will discuss the needs of the novice, as the more experienced investigator will probably already have a good idea of what is needed. The apprentice will learn, but only after taking hundreds, then thousands of photographs with his training equipment.

So what camera should the beginner get? First, as when purchasing any equipment, check to see if someone in your family has a camera. Remember, Uncle Fred had the binoculars; see if he has a camera. Second, in looking to buy one, check the classified ads in your newspapers for used photographic equipment. Your first one should be a single-lens reflex (SLR) camera that requires you to work all of the settings. No auto-exposer, no auto-focus, and no auto-winder. This will not be a new camera. Most single-lens reflex cameras have several automatic features that, if used, prevent you from learning the basics of photography that I feel you should know. And learning the basics is the key to good photography.

In the 1970s, there was an explosion in the photography industry. The SLR became truly affordable to the average person who was interested in photography. A lot of people spent a lot of money for cameras they could not use. Most had some automatic features, but nothing like today. The majority of people put these cameras away or traded them for simpler models. These people did not want to take the time to learn the basics of photography and only wanted good pictures. They found that the simple, cheap camera did the job most of the time. The simple camera couldn't do everything, but you didn't have to work to take photos, either. Most people did not realize that with just a little effort spent learning how to use their SLRs properly they could take great photos and in almost every condition and situation. Eventually, as an investigator, you will be required to take photographs of something the average camera or amateur photographer cannot. That said, go get one of these cameras.

Next, if the camera does not have a built-in light meter, get one. Old ones are practically given away. New ones can be expensive or cheap. The more expensive light meters will have one or two extra features that may be nice to have later but are not necessary when you are learning photography.

Although not essential, a tripod is nice to have. Again, there are used ones out there if you look for them. These can range from the cheap in price and quality to the very expensive—sometimes costing more than what you paid for a used camera.

Most cameras come with a lens. This may seem like a dumb statement, but, believe it or not, today the lenses on new cameras are often priced separately from the body of the camera. The lens is what bends the light as it enters the camera. It also, in one way, controls the amount of light that enters. These two main functions are the bases of the two features referred to most often when discussing lenses.

Focal Length

The first of these features is focal length. The focal length is the distance from a primary element in the front of the lens of the camera to the film plane. The film plane is the location in the back of the camera where the film is pulled out of its cassette to a position in line with the lens and held there. The film is in this position when it is exposed (when you press the button and take the picture). Many times on the top of the camera body there will be a circle with a line going through it, indicating where inside the camera the film plane is. On a regular 35mm SLR, a normal lens is one that has a focal length of roughly 40mm to 55mm. Without going into great detail, this lens will produce an image that gives the best representation of the view of the human eye for that film size. Just what does that mean? First, most people know what it is like to look through a telescope. A telescopic image does not represent the way you and I normally see. To the other extreme, most people have seen a photo that was taken with a wide-angle lens, wherein the things that are closest to the lens appear disproportionately larger and things that are farther away quickly become smaller, creating a ballooning effect. The normal lens records the image the way we normally view things, not the way telescopic or wide-angle lenses do.

The more the focal length of the lens drops below the normal range, the more profound this ballooning effect becomes. Most common wide-angle lenses are 28mm or 35mm. There are shorter lenses, but those beyond 28mm are considerably more expensive and are not really necessary for most people, let alone PIs. The 28mm lens, in my opinion, is probably the best and shortest wide-angle lens for the private detective to have in his camera bag (that is, when you have a camera bag and start filling it with lenses and gadgets). When used properly, the 28mm lens will obviously give you a wide-angle view of your subject or object with minimal distortion. PHOTO TIP: When using a wide-angle lens, keep your camera as level as possible and your subject or object a reasonable distance away. Otherwise, the distortion of the wide-angle lens will be more apparent and you will not get the best rendition.

Wide-angle distortion is not always apparent to the trained eye, but it can be annoying. The next time you are at the local supermarket waiting in line to buy munchies for your next stakeout or surveillance, pick up one or two of the tabloid newspapers on display. Get the ones that usually have color photos of celebrities. The photographer is usually fighting a crowd around the celebrity and trying to get as much of the celebrity in the picture as possible. In this case, the photographer uses a wide-angle lens. Study these pictures. Notice how when the photographer is right in the subject's face the image becomes distorted. The editors usually use this kind of photo if they want to upset the movie star for one reason or another. If the photographer get a full-length shot with a wide-angle lens, the body appears to bend unnaturally. The face and shoulders seem okay, but the lower part of the body and feet, even though in the photo, strangely move away from you. As a private investigator, if you use a wide-angle lens, you want your image to be an accurate rendition of your subject and not one that is offensive to your visual senses.

Now, when you want to get closer visually but remain at a safe distance and keep your location unknown to your subject, consider the telephoto lens. When the focal length of the lens gets larger than that of a normal lens, it will magnify or bring your subject closer. The longer the focal length, the stronger the magnification. Telescopes are described in terms of their power, and the "X" is used to indicate this (e.g., 4X represents a 4-power magnification, 10X represents a 10-power of magnification, and so on). In camera lenses, focal lengths are used to describe the strength of the lens in its magnification (e.g., 110mm, 200mm, 400mm, and up). The higher the number, the higher the magnification. This focal length is apparent in the visible size of the lens. Unlike most wide-angle lenses, which look very similar to normal camera lenses, telephoto lenses are apparent at first glance. They are physically longer and heavier. They also get in the way more.

Telephoto lenses also create a visual distortion in that they tend to flatten the image. This means that objects in the foreground or background will appear to be closer to your subject even though there is actually some distance between all of these elements. The best example of this is a photo of the moon very close to the horizon. The moon appears to fill the photo, and at the same time it appears closer to the earth and the houses or trees in the photo. The telephoto lens has flattened the image. This usually cannot be avoided, because your subject is picking his location and surroundings. But if you want to reduce this as much as possible, shoot your subject when he or she is closest to the background or other objects that will be in the picture.

Zoom lenses are not lenses that travel fast, unless you and your camera are flying somewhere on a jet. Okay, bad play on words. The zoom lens is one on which working focal length varies. By either turning or sliding an extra outer ring, you can change the focal length from maximum to minimum length or any length in between. An example of this would be a zoom lens that goes from 80mm to 210mm. Different zoom lenses have different ranges in terms of focal lengths. Zoom lenses are more expensive, but they do offer the flexibility of having the capabilities of several lenses in one.

Aperture

The second main feature of the lens is its aperture. This is usually listed as the widest opening capability of the lens and is given in f-stops. The f-stop is a number given to a specific size of opening in the lens for light to pass through. To the amateur the numbers used will seem strange, in that they do not represent actual measurements. They will also seem backward because the smaller number is used for an opening that lets in more light, and the larger numbers indicate a smaller opening.

I will attempt to tell you what the numbers mean in as few words as possible to give you an overview and a basic understanding. However, you will need to study the subject further to know what it all means. It is not difficult, but in my experience, some people take a little longer than others to grasp the concept. If you were good in math, it will probably be easier for you. If not, or if for whatever reason you just cannot grasp why f-stops are the way they are, don't worry. They work. It's like turning on a radio. You have some idea what's going on. You know it has to have a battery or be plugged in to have power. You have to turn it on and tune it to hear it. But if you opened it up, you probably would not know why it works. The same is true for f-stops. Most people will learn how to use them, but not why they are the size they are or why those particular numbers are used.

F-stops are expressed in numbers that represent a ratio of the size of the aperture opening and the focal length of the lens. This is the only way to measure the amount of light that is passing through the lens that is consistent with every lens, no matter its focal length. Examples of specific f-stop numbers are 2, 2.8, 4, 5.6, 8, 11, 16, and 22. Notice that every other number roughly doubles, in value. Yet as you go from f-2 to f-2.8, the amount of light that passes through the lens is cut in half. The number may not seem to make sense, but it works. In the beginning, just think of each f-stop as a point that either lets in twice as much light or half as much light as the f-stop next to it. In my experience, if you do not understand this right away, as you continue to learn more about photography and how to meter light and set the f-stops and shutter speed, you will find that one day what it all means will hit you. I believe that while it is helpful to understand the math involved in all of this, it is not necessary to go crazy over it.

Mounting

There must be a marriage between the body of the camera and the lens, and this is the mounting. This will be configured differently depending on the maker. Most cameras today have a bayonet-type mount where you line the lens up to a mark on the camera and then twist, push in, and give it a short turn until it clicks in place. Some older-model lenses will just screw on the camera. You must be careful, though, that the lens has the proper mounting for the camera you use.

Even various models that are manufactured by the same company will have different mounting configurations.

As I stated before, the body of your camera should be completely manual in its operation. Only that way will you really learn how to use your camera, and, in reality, almost any camera, no matter what format, size, make, and manufacture. There will be some minor differences in cameras, but these will consist primarily of special automatic features that can be learned quickly. Only after using a manual camera will you truly appreciate automatic features later on. You will also learn to do without them when they fail or their batteries fail. Over the last 20 years, the camera, particularly the 35mm, has evolved significantly. More automated features, dependent on batteries, have become available. The electronics, computer chips, and the miniaturization of parts have created truly amazing cameras. But like anything else, the more extras there are in a camera, the more things that can go wrong with it. When one of these many new features breaks down in the field, there is not much you can do. Consider yourself lucky if it is just the battery. Batteries also are better than they were just a few years ago, but by their own definition, they are just a storage device. They eventually run out of power. But as a good PI, naturally, you will have spare batteries in your camera bag. There are some cameras with some minor automated features so that if your batteries fail you can still operate the camera manually. If you can get one of these, great, but remember to learn how to use it manually first.

Accessories
Once you have your camera, several lenses, and a tripod, you will soon discover the wonderful world of gadgets. There are more gadgets and accessories for photographers than you could ever imagine, until you get your first photo supply catalog. When you do, you will think you need them all. You don't. Do not become a photo gadget junkie. Always think twice before buying gadgets. Can what you want to do be

done without it? Will it really help, save you time, or save you money? Think.

VIDEO

Let's move on to video. The camera you should get is the one that will be out next week. The camera you should use is the one you can get your hands on. Home video has been around for more than 25 years. It became financially reasonable in the last 10 years. Like computers, video cameras are changing and getting better every day. They are smaller, easier to use, and less expensive, and give a higher-quality of image. Tomorrow they will be better yet.

Since the home video camera has only been around for a reasonably short period of time, you won't find many just sitting in some uncle's closet. If you can borrow one as needed, great. If you can get one secondhand at a good price, great. But don't invest too much in a used one, because new ones are not that expensive and will usually be a lot better than those made just last year.

As I stated before, the main difference between a video and a still camera is that with the former you will be recording movement. Usually this should not be camera movement (which is the most common mistake people make in using video cameras), but rather the movement of your subject. The only time the camera should move is to follow the subject when he or she begins to move out of the frame of the picture.

The second biggest mistake in using a video camera is too much zooming. Almost all personal video cameras have zoom lenses. When first using a video camera, everyone likes to zoom in and out. I was no different. Play with the camera for a while with family and friends and get rid of that desire. Once you watch the tapes, you will see how much it detracts from what you are doing. There are proper times to zoom in or out, dictated by the event. They are the exceptions, however, not the rule.

65

Unless you are already doing a lot of surveillance or evidence photography, do not spend a lot of money until you find out what you really need. If you discover you are doing a lot of surveillance in, for instance, workman's compensation cases, long lenses will be necessary, but it is not likely that you will need a close-up lens or a camera that mounts to a microscope. On the other hand, if you find you are doing evidence work, the latter features may be necessary. If you have to, borrow or rent the equipment as necessary and buy only when it becomes cost-effective. For some time, most of my work did not require me to use a video camera, and therefore I would borrow one only when I needed it. Eventually, I did get a case that required substantial video work, and then I did purchase a video camera. It took me 12 years to get one, and it was only after considerable evaluation.

OTHER CONSIDERATIONS

Several things were not discussed extensively in this chapter that deserve some mention.

Film Development

The first is film. In the old school of police photography, everything was shot on black-and-white film. You also had to know how to develop film, enlarge, and print images. Today, with one-hour processing for color film, black and white would seem to be a thing in the past. In spite of this, I highly recommend taking a formal course on black-and-white film development and print making. As you learn these things, you will learn more about how to take better pictures. You will also learn how the image can be manipulated. This is important to know if you have to evaluate a photograph to get information from it.

Computer Manipulation

The computer power that was used to put a man on the moon in July of 1969 is now used to play video games, control microwave ovens, and help me write this book on my desktop computer. Who knows for sure what the computer will be able to do to photographs and videos in the very near future. It will be up to you, at a minimum, to be aware of these capabilities.

Today, computer manipulation of images is becoming easier, to the point that it can be almost impossible—if not impossible—to detect. This is a growing science that will create problems and also opportunities for private detectives. Since Louis J.M. Daguerre developed photography in 1837, others almost immediately began developing ways of manipulating the picture. By today's standards, these manipulations were very crude, and almost anyone can detect them. But today, with computer technology, not only are images just slightly changed, whole new images are created. Just look at the movies in the last several years, for example, *Jurassic Park* and *Forrest Gump*. For each, the producers created things, events, people, and creatures that do not exist. Each contains things that appear real but are not. This kind of technology will create problems for investigators as we gather information to record and report it. What we record may be disputed by a manipulated photograph. There will be those who will change information (that is, create a deception) to suit their needs. The detective will have to understand the basics of how these manipulations are achieved and what the latest capabilities are in these manipulations—or know experts who will be able to detect them.

Along the same lines, video can be manipulated. With Hollywood special effects creating the impossible and making it look real, you can expect those capabilities to be on the high school computer.

• • • • •

To conclude this chapter, let me just say that your knowledge and experience will do more for you than the tools you use. Learn from your mistakes. When photos don't turn out the way you planned, ask an expert to tell you what you did wrong. You need the right tools for the job, but if you don't know how to use them, they're worthless. Only after you have learned to use what you already have to the best of both your abilities and the tools' capabilities should you take the step to purchase new equipment.

ASSIGNMENTS

1. Learning photography does take money—for film, cameras, and other equipment. If you do not have these, make a list of what basic equipment you need. Visit a local camera store to get ideas. Price these items at the store and in the classified ads of the newspaper. Put this information in your notebook.

2. Get a book on basic photography and study it. (See the Bibliography for the two books I recommend for basic and advanced study.)

3. From what you understand about private detectives at this point, write down as many things as you can about how you think private detectives use video and photography.

CHAPTER EIGHT

FIREARMS

In the make-believe world of novels, TV, and movies, the private detective and guns seem inseparable. In every story, the PI usually has one or two shootouts. If every one of these tales were to be believed, you, as a private detective, would go through bullets like similes in a Mickey Spillane novel. It's what sells in books and in the theaters. However, it's not what it is like in the real world. This is not to say that guns are not needed or used by PIs. The reality is that although many PIs carry guns, rarely do they ever use them to shoot at someone.

Let's first look at what a gun is. Whether it be a long gun, (such as a rifle or shotgun) or a handgun, automatic, or revolver, its primary purpose must be understood completely and absolutely. A gun is a tool, and the purpose of that tool is to kill. It must be understood that anytime the owner of this tool decides to use it, he or she must be *justified* and *mentally ready* to take a life. Again, *anytime you fire a gun, you must be lawfully justified and mentally prepared to live with the fact that you have shot and killed someone.* Commit that last sentence to memory.

Naturally, I am not talking about target shooting and practicing the proper and safe use of a firearm. Learning how to handle a gun safely and proficiently and practice-shooting at a qualified firing range are the first things anyone who decides to own a gun must do. The concept of "point and shoot" is a simple one and is basic to firing a handgun, but that is reducing it to its simplest form. There are rules of safety regarding all aspects of guns: for having a gun, for firing a gun, for carrying a gun, for storing a gun There are more rules for gun safety and proper gun handling than I can list here. But as someone who has been around guns literally all of my life, I have learned the importance and necessity of gun safety. Jeff Cooper, a noted gun expert, states the basic rules better than most others, myself included, in his *General Pistol Manual*. They are as follows:

1. All guns are always loaded. No exceptions. Don't pretend. Be deadly serious about it and we will never again hear that sheeplike bleat, "But I didn't know it was loaded!"
2. Never let the muzzle cover anything you are not willing to destroy. This rule is conspicuously and continuously violated and excused because "it was not loaded." (See rule #1.)
3. Keep your finger off the trigger until your sights are on the target. You cannot line up any faster than you can position your trigger finger, and there is no need to fire an unaligned piece.
4. Be sure of your target. Know what it is, what is in line with it, and what is behind it. Never shoot at anything that you have not positively identified.

If it is your choice to have a gun, you must also make the choice to learn and abide by these rules.

Some private detectives carry guns. Some do not. In most states there are laws regarding who can carry concealed weapons. Some states do not allow PIs to carry guns concealed. In some states, private detectives are subject to still more restrictions or are prohibited from even carrying a firearm. Other states may be more lenient. It will be your responsibility to find out what the laws are where you live. There are numerous books on the gun laws for all states, but what is listed in a book must be confirmed and clarified.

What is written in legalese may not be entirely clear to the police, the local district attorney, or even the state attorney general. You will have to research how the laws are enforced and what the legal opinions are regarding them. The laws may be clear and straightforward where you live, but the reality is that in some places, the way the law is enforced is not an accurate reflection of what the law actually is. You must learn what rights you have in your state in case you encounter local or other authorities who wish to infringe upon those rights.

Another reality is that even though it is legally feasible to obtain a concealed weapons permit, it may not be possible. In some states the laws are set up to discourage application for such a permit. And even if you do apply, the granting authorities are often deadset against allowing anyone to have such a permit, and rejecting these applications is left to their discretion. This is not right or fair, but it is the way it is, and we as lawfully licensed PIs must live with these inequities until they change.

Now, if you find you are permitted to carry a firearm and decide that you do want to, you had better learn all about firearms first. (From this point on, when I speak of firearms, I will be referring to handguns.) If you know nothing about them, learn from someone who knows. Better yet, learn from someone who is a certified instructor. On your own, there are a number of things you can learn without even picking up a gun. But this cannot replace the hands-on training necessary to be proficient with firearms.

Your research should begin with the two general types of handguns that are out there, i.e., the revolver and the automatic. Their names describe the physical characteristics of how the bullets are set in the action of the gun to be fired. The automatic reloads a cartridge into the chamber and recocks the action so it can be fired again by just a pull of the trigger. Either recoil of the fired cartridge or the burned gases recirculated back into the chamber is what forces the action back to reload it. A revolver uses the force of the pull of the trigger or the pulling back of the hammer to turn the cylinder to line up a cartridge with the barrel to be fired. A continuation of the pull of the trigger releases the hammer on the cartridge and fires the weapon. Again, the hammer or trigger is pulled back to align a new cartridge. Although there are numerous models of automatics and revolvers, once you've examined them, you will see that there are certain similarities between all revolvers and all automatics.

There are other kinds of handguns, but they are not generally considered primary sidearms. For example, I am sure you have heard of derringers. Derringer is now a generic name for a very small single- or double-barreled handgun. The derringer comes in many calibers and is carried as a backup piece by some detectives and police officers. For many PIs, its small size but limited round capacity makes it suitable for carrying as a backup but never as a primary gun. Another handgun that is definitely not meant as a concealed firearm is one that has bolt action. This action is one that is usually used primarily for rifles. This type of gun is very powerful—in fact, too powerful and too large to be used in the everyday life of a PI.

In picking a sidearm, you must also pick a caliber. Although the caliber generally refers to the diameter of the bullet fired, it also encompasses several other factors, such as the length of the cartridge, the date of adoption, or the proprietor or designer. For example, 30-06 indicates that the bullet has an approximate diameter of .30 inches and the year it was adopted as a standard rifle cartridge was 1906. A .45 ACP tells you that the caliber is .45 inches for the Automatic Colt Pistol. Further, 9mm "Luger" or "Parabellum" would indicate a German-design caliber. This is different than the 9mm "Browning short" (more commonly known as the .380 ACP), which is also a European design but with American adaptation. Each has differences that are significant to that particular caliber.

Now at this point, the construction of the calibers and

cartridge can get very confusing. The weight of the bullet can vary within the same caliber. Bullets of the same weight and size can be used in different cartridges and calibers. Several calibers can fire the same bullet, but what varies is the length of their casings, which permits a weapon to hold more or less gunpowder. For example, the 9mm automatic fires the same diameter bullet as the .380 automatic. The shell casing is longer on the 9mm; hence, it has a more powerful cartridge and faster bullet. A .357 Magnum revolver can shoot both .357 Magnum and .38 Special cartridges, but a .38 Special handgun cannot shoot a .357 Magnum cartridge. Minor points to note will be the shape of the rear of the cartridge and the way it is held in place in the chamber. On most automatics, the rear of the casing is flush with the rest of it. On most revolvers, the rear of the casing has a small ridge that extends slightly beyond the rest of the sides of the casing.

Now comes the six-million-dollar question. If you choose to carry a firearm, what should it be? Ask one PI what kind of gun he likes and you will get one answer. Ask the next PI and he may give you another. Ask a police officer, and he may say you should only carry a certain type and caliber. Talk to a federal agent, and you will probably get another opinion. Is there a correct answer? What is the best gun? What caliber?

As for this investigator, I can offer several rules of thumb that will lead you to your own correct answer. For most PIs, if the decision is made to carry a handgun, it will have to be concealed (with proper permits). The next criterion to consider is its stopping power. The fact is that if you must use a gun, it should be as effective as possible. This means that whatever you carry and use must not only be able to hit the subject but put him down and out with one shot. You may not get a chance for a second. *Please note that this is not absolute, nor is it guaranteed.* There are numerous other factors involved in determining stopping power. Even the length of the barrel will affect the ballistics of the cartridge and its effectiveness in putting down an assailant. *There is no way I, or anyone else, can guarantee that any gun will stop anyone absolutely with just one shot.* The attacker's physical condition, his size, and whether he is on any drugs can all have a dramatic effect on any weapon's stopping power. One more time: *there is no guarantee that just because you've shot someone he will no longer be a threat.*

The weapon you choose should be reliable and naturally accurate. To most experts in the field, extralarge-capacity magazines (often mistakenly referred to as clips) are less important than caliber. On guns with large magazines, you are usually using a smaller and—according to many experts —less efficient cartridge.

If you are a beginner, you will probably learn with a smaller caliber just to gain experience with guns. As you progress, you will gain proficiency and accuracy. If you step up to a large caliber, you may find it uncomfortable and, depending on the gun, even painful. You will be tempted to fall back to the smaller caliber. Don't. You want to maintain proficiency with the small gun, but it is essential that you advance to the most effective weapon that you can carry and shoot. Now is not the time to stop the learning process or your training. If a situation arises that forces you to defend yourself or someone else, you must do so with a weapon that will do the job and with the skills and ability necessary to make it do its job.

Okay already—what caliber should you carry? My answer is nothing smaller than a .57 Magnum, a 10mm or .40 caliber, or a .45 ACP. These calibers offer the best stopping power of most handguns.

There has always been and always will be a debate over which is better—the revolver or the automatic. Revolvers rarely, if ever, jam. Automatics can jam, but they can be reloaded faster. Both can have excellent stopping power.

As you progress in your training you should make it your goal to learn about not just handguns but most types of firearms. The more you know about guns in general, the more you will respect their power. This power—what they are capable of doing in someone's hand—must always be respected. A gun in the wrong hands or improperly handled is extremely dangerous. This must never be forgotten. A gun in the hand of someone who understands its capabilities and exercises safe gun handling is less likely to be involved in an accidental discharge. Remember, a bullet, once fired, does not change its course or stop. So, from me to you, *let's not have any bullet go anyplace unintended or go through or stop anyplace it's not meant to be.*

If you have never had any gun training or experience, don't buy a gun, any gun, until you have had adequate firearms training and instruction in gun safety. To get training, check with local sports associations, gun and sporting shops, colleges, and police agencies; county park education programs; and state wildlife management agencies. The National Rifle Association (NRA) is a resource with which just about everyone is familiar. For young people, it offers gun safety programs through local schools upon request. It also offers gun training by certified instructors throughout the year and across the country, many times sponsored by local sporting and gun clubs. If you are serious about carrying a firearm and understanding all firearms and their use, I highly recommend joining the NRA. There are numerous other gun organizations and shooting clubs, both local and national, which benefit the marksman and the apprentice PI alike. These will help you in your quest to learn about firearms as well as in becoming more proficient in their use.

There are dozens of magazines at your local bookstore on guns and shooting. In your local library there are numerous books on guns—their use, history, safety, and politics. The magazines will introduce you to what's new in guns, the latest laws, and available accessories, and they will also offer commentary on all aspects of gun use. Buy a few at the newsstand and then subscribe to the ones you like and that most suit your needs. If you become involved in the politics of gun ownership, the magazines will best keep you up to date with your rights.

If you choose to own a firearm, there are two other things you should do. The first is to purchase a gun-cleaning kit. Learn to clean and take care of your sidearm. It is not difficult. This will help you maintain not only its value, but, more importantly, its reliability. A rusty gun not only looks bad, but it could fail when you need it most. The second and final thing you must do is always keep your ammo fresh. Target shoot your oldest ammo first and keep your gun loaded with new ammo when on your side. Old ammunition is very unreliable and can misfire. Don't let it happen to you; it could be fatal.

This chapter is not the definitive on what there is to know about firearms. There is much more you will have to learn on your own. If you choose to own, carry, and possibly use a gun, you are obligated to learn all you can about its safe and proper use. That said, begin by doing the following assignments, but never stop learning more.

ASSIGNMENTS

1. Visit your local library or gun/sport shop and get a copy of your state and local gun laws. Make note of which sections and subsections of the law apply to gun ownership where you live.

2. Write down the section and subsections of the law that apply to the carrying of concealed weapons by private citizens.

3. Write down the section and subsections of the law that apply to private detectives. Please note that since each state has different laws regarding firearms, you may or may not find information available that corresponds to each of the topics you've been assigned to research here. These laws also may not all be in the same grouping of laws. You will need to search indexes or seek advice from those people or agencies that are well

informed on the laws, e.g., gun salespeople, police officers, and sheriff's departments.

4. Through discussion with those in authority (i.e., the county district attorney or, by his or her authority, the local sheriff or police chief), write a brief paragraph on what each of these laws means. Keep this in your notebook.

5. Obtain a copy of a gun safety pamphlet from a local gun store. Study it thoroughly. Keep it in your notebook.

6. By either visiting a local gun shop or attending a class taught by a qualified instructor, familiarize yourself with the two major types of handguns and learn how they operate. Review the basics of gun safety.

7. This last assignment on firearms is the most important: always remember the potential of guns, and when in their presence, think.

CHAPTER NINE

IMAGE

As you learned in the previous chapters, there are several specialized skills you will need to master as you launch a career as a private investigator. But if you go into business for yourself, understand that you are more than a PI—you are also a business person, an entrepreneur. As such, you will need to develop not only skills specific to the craft of private investigation but the marketing savvy required to make your business a success. Before you can market yourself and your services, you must think about cultivating an image.

You might ask, "So what's wrong with the way I look?" If you do so with some indignation, the answer may be, "More than you care to admit." We all like to believe that the way we dress and present ourselves is a statement of who we are and should be accepted as such. Maybe this is the way things should be. I emphasize the *maybe*. True, people should not judge us negatively just by the way we look. But the fact of life is that many people do judge us partly or wholly on the way we look. You can rant and rave about how unjust this is and vow never to do it yourself, but others still will to some degree or another.

Your *image*. That is what this is all about. One way or another, consciously or subconsciously, we all project an image of ourselves. A young man may grow his hair longer to play in a heavy metal band. A minister wears a clerical collar so people will recognize him as such. A truck driver who believes he's the modern-day cowboy might wear a cowboy hat and boots. Some chefs wear a tall white hat that's puffed and pleated at the top. In each of these examples, the person's appearance projects a certain image.

If I showed you a man with a pipe, a deerstalker's hat, and a magnifying glass, most of you would think of a very famous detective, Sherlock Holmes. If I showed you a woman in a black robe holding a gavel, I hope you would think of a judge. People will make judgments about who you are and what you do—and many times how well you do it—based on your clothes and appearance. I alluded to this earlier, but to reiterate, if you needed a doctor to treat you for a critical condition, would you go to one whose voice still cracked occasionally and looked like he might be just out of junior high school or one that had a few gray hairs and spoke to you with a reassuring voice? It is a safe bet that you would probably choose the older one. Some of you may say you would give the younger one a chance, but I ask you—would you really? Remember, your condition is critical and you want the best. Human nature dictates that first impressions will help you choose your doctor. You will want to feel reassured as soon as possible. The older doctor is more likely to give you that assurance. This may seem unfair to the younger doctor, and in some ways it is. But, since you are paying for it, shouldn't you have that choice (assuming we don't have nationalized medicine by the time this book comes out)?

I used a doctor as an example, but you could substitute beautician. Do you think your grandmother wants or should have to go to a beautician who has spiked purple hair? Her granddaughter may want to, and the beautician may be well qualified, but she probably will not get Grandma's money. Think back on when you have recently decided to use people's services. You'll probably recall that you were not comfortable with some of them, and even though you will not want to admit it, that probably had something to do with the way those people looked and the image they projected to you at the time.

Here is one more way to look at how image plays an important part in making a purchase. Suppose you were looking into buying a duck. If you saw a bird that had a chicken beak, would you buy it? Probably not. Maybe it just had a deformed beak. The next bird you saw was closer, but it barked like a dog. You would think it was a strange bird, but not a duck. Next, maybe you know what duck droppings look like and you found a bird just about right, but it didn't crap (see, no real bad language here) like a duck. You would move on. Finally, you see a bird that looks like a duck, talks like a duck, and squats like a duck. It's probably a duck, so you spend your money. The same thing is true when people want to pay for professional services. If you walk, talk, and present yourself as a professional, people's first impression is that you are that professional. This is the first part of making the sale. The goods are you and your services. Now get real close and remember this: *no money is made until the sale is made.* Let me repeat that: *no money is made until the sale is made.* In the business world, the salesperson is the only one who brings in the money. You must be a salesperson at all times, like it or not.

TAKE A CLOSE LOOK AT YOURSELF

Now that I have been repetitive for so long, let's get to the point. Go to a mirror. Try to find a good-sized one. Step back and take a good look. What do you see? Would you trust that person with your life? Yes, your life. Believe it or not, many of the people who will come to you for your services will be entrusting, in whole or in part, their lives with you. Whether this is true or not does not matter. The fact is that they believe it does.

Back to what you see in the mirror. Let's be a little analytical. First, do you have any physical faults? Change what you can; accept what you cannot. It is as simple as that. Again, like it or not, beauty sells. If you are born with good looks, count your blessings. If you can straighten a few crooked teeth, do it when you can afford it. If you should lose a few pounds, do the best you can. If some of you have to put on a few pounds, make them muscle. If there is something you don't like that you cannot do anything about, move on and don't think about it again. Since there is nothing you can do about it, worrying or complaining about it is a complete waste of time and energy. It will also create unhappiness, and nobody likes an unhappy private detective. All kidding aside, learn to live with it and just get on with your life.

Now, head to toe, fingertip to fingertip, how's your grooming? Yes, grooming. Are you clean? Is your hair cut (guys, don't worry about length now)? Is it brushed or combed? Are your fingernails trimmed and clean? Men, are you clean-shaven or is your beard or mustache trimmed? Women, how's your makeup? Does it flatter you?

These are all tough questions. Sometimes you will not be able to answer them. You may have to ask a close friend who will be totally truthful in his or her evaluation of you. This person must be willing to tell you anything about your appearance that others might find offensive and that you can correct. This includes things that could convey that you may not pay careful attention to your appearance or personal hygiene. At first this evaluation will probably be very painful. More painful may be the realization that people may have known and said things about you in the past because of these personal shortcomings.

Now that I have possibly destroyed what was left of your self-esteem, it's time to do something about it. List all of the things you can do something about. Now start writing down what you can do about them. Write down as many ideas as you can. When you're done, share your list with that special friend. See if she or he can give you some more ideas. Write them down. Now, decide which of these ideas might really make a positive change in you. What things can you do starting now, today, to make these changes? Now you're going to write these things down and make them part of your personal improvement "Goals List." You can write them on a 3" x 5" card and make two columns. At the top put MY APPEAR-ANCE. In the first column, write those things or "goals" that you want to and can change about yourself. In the second column, list those things or "actions" that will help you make these changes. Be brief in your descriptions; you'll know what they mean. They are just there to remind you every day of what you need to do to make these changes. If you review these goals and actions consistently, every day (more than once if possible), they will begin to become part of your subconscious mind.

At first you will have to think about when and where you can do these things. As you review the list, you may have to actually plan when to do some of them and make a conscious effort to do them. It will not be easy, nor will it feel natural to do it this way, but it works. Anytime something substantial is done, it usually begins with an idea and a plan of action. Make that plan a part of your everyday life. Remember, you are making changes to make a better you. You are still you, but you are growing inside, which will bring about changes within and on the outside. Choose positive changes and work toward them constantly. They will reward you in more ways than I can describe here. One thing I will say, though, is that if you make a conscious effort to look your best, not out of vanity but because of pride in yourself, you will not only do better in anything you undertake, but you will feel better about your life. High self-esteem is not your only goal in life, but it is a very important one.

HOW ARE YOUR CLOTHES?

Now I'm getting personal. That's the way some people feel about their clothes. Criticize someone's clothes and you've started a fight. So what's wrong with your clothes? Nothing, maybe. Again, remember that you will be judged by your appearance. Certain clothes are appropriate for certain times and places. When it's time to be professional, it's time to dress like a professional. Whether as a private detective or some other type of professional, you will have a uniform of sorts. That uniform will consist of dressing like a professional business person.

What do professional business people wear? How will you know what is acceptable? What does a man or woman wear as a professional private detective? I am not talking about when you are out in the field doing surveillance or working a case that takes you into the middle of a cow field to get the best view of some strange accident. I am referring to when you are dealing with other professionals such as attorneys, judges, doctors, private business people, and your clients. The first time any one of these people meets you is probably the most important. I did not say the first time *you* see *him or her*, and there is a difference. You are not spending money with the client, but rather he or she with you. Again, the client will want that visual assurance.

First, what does a private investigator wear at these times? Simply the best he or she can afford. Your clothes are among your most valuable image-building tools. They help you get and keep clients. And remember, clients are the ones who pay you. For men, this means suits, sport coats, dress slacks, quality ties, and good-looking, polished shoes. For women, it's suits, blouses, skirts, quality hose, and proper shoes. In other words, wear clothes that look like business clothes, not the latest fashion trend. Style over fad. Stability over chaos.

Among the best examples private detectives can follow are attorneys. What do the most successful attorneys wear in your area? A sure bet is that they shop at a quality clothing store and not the local discount store. They probably spend three to four times the amount of money you now spend for a suit or outfit, and it is not just because they have the money. It is because they know clients expect them to look successful, and, yes, to even look expensive. Next, find out where most of the lawyers go to buy their clothes. Depending on the size of your community, there may be several stores or just a few of them, but there will be ones that stand out from the rest. Visit these stores when they are not too busy and look around. If a store clerk offers assistance, accept it. Tell him what you are doing—namely that you are not just shopping but looking to make major changes in your current wardrobe. Let him know that although you are not prepared to make any major purchases at this time, you plan to in the very near future. Men and women should both find out what makes a good suit. Men, ask about different shirts, their collars, fabric, and the different cuffs. Women, look at quality blouses and the different styles. What kind goes best with suits and skirts? What types of jackets are acceptable in different business settings? What do lawyers wear in court? Ask questions. What would look good on you? Look at prices for both off-the-rack and custom-made clothes. Let them take your measurements and keep them on file (tell your family and friends to buy you Christmas or birthday gifts there).

Before you buy, something else you can do is read up on what makes a difference in what you wear. There are several books on dressing for success. Check some out of your local library or purchase some at a bookstore in your area and read them. Keep in mind that some of what they say will be dated, as will the fashions shown. There are several magazines that are targeted to professionals, their life-styles, their clothes, and how they take care of their bodies. Get several, read them, and learn.

Now, with this newfound knowledge on personal attire, you are somewhat prepared to put together your new wardrobe. Whether you're a man or woman, the first thing you should get when you can afford it is a quality suit. If you can afford only one suit, take care of it. When you don't need to wear the coat, take it off and hang it up. Don't lounge in the suit pants or skirt when you're not working. Always hang your suit up properly when you are not wearing it, and when it needs cleaning, get it dry-cleaned. Remember, if this is your only suit, it is a tool that is not to be abused. If you do all of this, it will serve you well.

After you buy the suit, get the basics in quality shirts, blouses, and other accessories. As moneys permit, build your wardrobe to suit the seasons and occasions. Dress shoes should be well maintained and polished as needed. Stay with accessories that flatter an outfit but do not clutter it.

Imagine you want a new fast car. You look at two that can both go as fast as you want. One looks like a box with wheels, and the other looks as if it is ready to take off. The best bet is that you would choose the one that *looks like* it's fast. Clients want the same thing and are willing to pay more for it.

ASSIGNMENTS

1. Go to a quality clothing store and learn what a classic suit is. Next, with the help of a clothing professional, determine which suit looks best on you and is one that you can afford. Once this is done, do what you have to do (legally) to get the money necessary and buy it.

2. Look at your shoes. If they do not match your new suit, get new shoes also. Next, spend just a little more money for a shoe-polishing kit and learn how to use it. If the shoes cannot be polished, they can be cleaned. Learn the ways that can be done.

3. When you visit your local quality clothing store, ask to be put on its mailing or calling list so that you will be notified when it is having its next trunk sale on suits. It will save you money.

CHAPTER TEN

WHERE DO CLIENTS COME FROM?

Once you have cultivated an image, you are ready to begin marketing your business and your services to potential clients. Clients—your bread and butter. The people who are going to pay to use your services. Where are they, and where do they come from? The simple answer is, they are out there. But, you ask, where is "out there"? Again, very simple. Everywhere out there.

Okay, maybe I am being a little off-the-wall with you, but it is still true. The money you will earn will come from people out in the real world. It could be your neighbor, a friend, business people with whom you have dealt, store and shop owners whose businesses you have patronized, and people you do not know now. In reality, anyone and everyone may be a client someday. They may not need us today, tomorrow, next week, or even next year, but they are likely to sometime in the future. Some will need the services of a PI right away. Others will need us several times in their lives. Some professionals will use our services over and over, but only when they really need us.

As a general rule, people do not "impulse" buy the services of a PI. That is, they do not walk down the street and see a sign that says, "SALE, THIS WEEK ONLY, DOMESTIC INVESTIGATIONS," and then dash in and put their money down to check on a cheating spouse. Most of the time people have to think long and hard about retaining the services of the PI. Every once in a while someone will call a PI prematurely, but it is not common. The point of this is that a PI's services are a bit like those of a doctor: you usually only call one when you are sick or when you need some preventative medicine. Most of what you will do as a PI will be to help someone after something has already happened. It could be a domestic problem, a civil dispute, criminal detection or defense, or the desire to locate someone for a number of reasons. But in all these cases, the person usually seeks the services of a PI only after something has occurred. However, once in a while a client may ask you to do some preventative work, such as investigating future partners, either in business or in life (premarital investigations). Don't laugh; this is a growing field. Most people do not marry the guy or girl next door, and they or their parents want to know a little more about the future spouse or son/daughter-in-law to be.

But back to where the clients are, or better put, how you find them. First, as I stated earlier, you must remember that in business, no money is made until the product or service is sold. You must market yourself—sell your services.

"*Sell?* But I want to be a private investigator, not a salesman," you're probably saying. OK, if you do not want to sell, go work for someone else in a factory assembly line, dig ditches, or go on welfare. If you do not want to sell, don't take any job that will bring you in contact with the public. Don't accept any position from which you might move up in any way. Forget about becoming any kind of manager, because once you get above a certain level in almost any job, occupation, trade, or profession, there is selling involved. That might mean selling a product, a service, or a concept or idea, as well as selling what you do as an individual. On a personal level, self-promotion is probably the most important kind of selling that you will ever do. Think of all the times in your life you had to sell yourself to get a job. Have you ever tried to convince someone to accept your point of view? That is selling an idea. Do not fool yourself by rationalizing that you have never sold yourself. In one way or another, everyone who has goals, dreams, and desires must sell. If you honestly feel that you do not have to sell, do not want to sell, or cannot sell, you have two choices: do something else, like menial labor, or change your way of thinking about selling.

By now I hope you realize that just about everyone does some kind of selling. Now I want you to learn to apply the selling you have been doing all your life to your career as a private detective. As I said earlier, people will not come to a private detective until they need one. When they do, you want that private detective to be you. But what will make you stand out and be recognized as a private investigator?

First, you must have a long-term concept of selling—that is, keeping your name out there in the community where you choose to work. The community can be geographical, such as your hometown and surrounding areas, or it can be defined by an area of need, such as the legal community. It can even be created by the specialized need for a service, such as arson investigation by insurance companies. Within all of these communities, there will be ways of obtaining and maintaining what is known as "name recognition."

Long before you may be needed, you let people know who and what you are—not just once, but many, many times. In the world of advertising it is said that, on the average, a person must hear something seven times before he or she will remember it. And that memory is not long, considering how many different advertisements people are bombarded with in just one day, in just one medium (TV, radio, newspaper, magazines). Just like all other businesses, you must fight for the minds of those potential clients. You will have to work at it, but you should work smart at it. That is why it is important that you learn about many of the different techniques to be used, the various media to choose from, the costs involved, and what does and doesn't work.

Long-term name recognition is an ongoing process—one that you will, in the beginning, have to think consciously about almost all the time. Everyone you meet must be considered a potential client. You must pass along your name and your business name to these people. When you are talking to professionals or other business people, exchange business cards. Read their cards and say their names. Ask how to pronounce a name if it is difficult. Find out about their business. Answer any questions you can about what you do. Remember to thank people for their time and remind them to call you if you can ever be of service.

Your strategy for building long-term name recognition must also include public relations. For the private investigator, it is a little more difficult to have "public relations," because what we are doing is private, but it can be done. If you are planning to do a lot of undercover work, don't plan on having your photo in the newspaper. But you can still get press coverage.

It would be impossible to give a complete PR program in the limited space of this book, but there are a number of books out there that deal in depth with the use of press releases. It will be up to you to discover their uses and possibilities.

Now, this is the easy part. Most PIs like to talk about who they are and what they are about. Most of the time when you meet people casually and they learn you are a private detective, they will ask questions. What is not so easy is going out into the real world to someone who has the strong possibility of becoming a client, such as a lawyer, and telling that person why you think he or she should hire you. In encounters such as this, all of your insecurities will surface. And, be forewarned, some of these potential clients will test you to the limits of these insecurities. Some will take pleasure in trying to bring you down and challenge you in everything you say or do. Many times—and *most* of the time in the beginning—it will be among the hardest things you will ever do. But if you have prepared yourself for the craft, prepared yourself to be an independent business person, and prepared yourself in your own mind, you will not only survive but prevail in the selling process.

This is not to say that you will start getting clients right and left and more work than you know what to do with. It means that you will see results if you are persistent. Understand up front that selling is also numbers. The first person you try to sell to may say no. The next one may say no. This may go on for what seems like forever, but as long as you persevere, the first sale will eventually happen . . . followed by a second, then a third, and so forth. If you meet and try to sell to enough people, you will make a sale.

Now that first sale may be a very small one, but it is still a start. With that first sale, you learn what you did right, and, likewise, with no sales, you learn what you did wrong. Remember, no money can come in until the sale is made. It is only by persisting, doing quality work, and continuing to learn the selling process that you will make future sales possible. After a while, the face-to-face selling process will become second nature to you. At times, the selling will become more fun than some of the work you will be asked to do.

The community in which you wish to work will also determine some of the means for selling. If you wish to have clients from the general public, obviously the yellow pages will be a prime source of obtaining them. It is a passive means of selling, in that the client must look for providers of a service first and then decide whom to use. But your ad is effective in reaching a very targeted audience: people who are in need of the specific product or service you offer. Plus, the more you offer in your ad, the more calls you will probably get. A note of caution here, though. If you plan to advertise directly to the general public, be prepared for whatever may come. You will get calls about every possible problem in the world, and this is not an exaggeration. Along with sincere people with real problems you will get your share of people whose biggest problem is what is between their ears, or what is not there. People will call you at all hours, seven days a week, with their problems. They will be persistent until they talk to you. Some will get angry if you don't give them the attention they want. Others will expect you to work for nothing, not understanding what it means to be a private detective. You will hear stories that are meant to break your heart and persuade you to get personally involved. Those with a cause will try to enlist you to help slay their dragons. In other words, you are going to get some calls that will drive you crazy.

The location of your business can also be an added part of your selling. If you work out of your home in a nice residential area, you probably will not get a lot of drive-by or walk-by recognition. If you have an office in the heart of a business district with a big eye painted on the front window, obviously you will draw more attention. I know of agencies that are located on main roads and have huge signs out front. This, along with their ads in the yellow pages, attract numerous calls from the general public. Some agencies have even opened offices inside shopping malls. They do get the advantage of a lot of walk-by traffic, but there is a downside to this. Some potential clients do not like to be seen coming and going from a PI's office. Imagine that a client leaves your office at the mall or downtown and is seen by the best friend of his or her spouse. The friend tells the spouse, who naturally wants to know what's going on. It could create some problems on the home front.

Your future clients could be relatives, friends, old schoolmates, or anyone they may know. Let all of these people know what you do for a living. Tell them that you are looking for clients. Someday they or one of their friends may need you. Also, remember that once you've done business with a client, that person can provide some of your best advertising. If the situation permits, past clients will tell others of your great work. Another important note here is that if you do a good job, a client will tell maybe 10 people. If you do a great job, the client will still tell only about 10 people. If you do a lousy job, your client will tell 50 people. Enough said.

Marketing to a specific group is one of the best ways of

getting work. If you want to do legal-type investigations, make yourself known to the lawyers. If you want to do arson investigations, become known to insurance companies. If you want to do theft and loss prevention, contact members of the retail and general business community. Adopt a multifaceted approach. In each of the organizations or groups you are targeting, find the people who are in charge of retaining the services of private detectives. Send them promotional information, then visit them and call them back to follow up. After you've done this once, wait an appropriate amount of time and do it again. If your services are specific, target and sell to those people who will need those services the most.

One last point of selling: "Show the sizzle, then sell the steak." Listing services or types of work done would seem logical in just about any advertising or sales pitch. But this alone is not going to make the sale. What works is selling, or what is going to benefit or please him or her. For example, in selling you a steak, a sales rep might say it comes from corn-fed cattle, aged and butchered by the best. If he or she then offers the steak to you at a reasonable price, it may get you interested. But the salesperson who shows you the steak being prepared, sizzling on the grill, and throwing off its aroma, and then tells you it is being done just for you is the one who will sell more steaks than anyone else. The point is, what will your product or service do for the clients you are targeting? How will they benefit? Will it make them look good? Will they feel better about themselves? Will it get them out of a bad situation? Sell the "sizzle" of your services. If you specialize in finding debtors, tell how the client can get some money. If you work for attorneys, tell how the information you provide will make them look good to their clients and make them more money. If you work for businesses in loss prevention and investigate thefts, show how they can save money and recover some losses. Show them the benefit and back it up by what you do.

ASSIGNMENTS

1. Look in your yellow pages. First, note how private detectives/investigators are listed. Second, find out if there is more than one heading under which they can be found. Which heading is used most? Now list the most outstanding features of the different ads.

2. Call or visit several of the agencies, explain that you are a student, and ask if they have any promotional material that you may have or look at.

3. Visit your library or a bookstore and get books on small business marketing and salesmanship or the art of selling. Read them.

4. Start a file folder for advertising, sales, and promotional ideas. After reading the books on marketing and salesmanship, start listing ideas as they come to you. Review them periodically and expand upon them. Start thinking like a salesperson.

5. List all the things or services you would like to offer as a private investigator in one column. In the next column, list the "sizzle" or the benefits of each.

CHAPTER ELEVEN

DON'TS

In the wonderful world of private detectives, there are many fun and exciting things to do. But there are some definite "no-nos" or "don't even think of doing its." How many times have you seen the Hollywood PI pull a lock pick out of his secret pocket or use some supersleuth listening device? Well, as much fun as it may seem to be able to pick a forbidden lock, bug a phone, or use a hidden mike to tape a conversation, it is almost always illegal.

Ever since I was a small boy I, too, have been fascinated by all of the PI's covert talents and abilities. As a teen, I began to read books on how to pick locks. I was a novice at electronics. With no malicious intent, I would explore places that were off limits to most people my age. My friends and I would plot, as if we were spies, ways to get in someplace without being detected. Again, it was never for personal gain or to take anything or hurt anyone, but just for the fun of it and to see if we could do it.

I never lost sight of the fact that most of what we planned would have been wrong to execute, even if we did not hurt anyone, damage anything, or take anything. However, I was still fascinated by these things. Eventually I did learn how to pick locks—and do it reasonably well. And I know more now than ever before about electronic eavesdropping. But I have never used these skills in any way that's remotely illegal.

My skills in picking locks are strictly personal. As a professional private detective, I have never picked a lock illegally. I did so legally for a client once. It was legal in that the lock was in the client's home. Without going into detail, the client had a legal right to have the lock opened. The client could have cut the lock off if he had wanted to, or we could have hired a locksmith to open it for us. I did it because it was expedient and he did not want it to be obvious that the lock had been opened. The point is that in all the time I have worked in public law enforcement and as a private detective, this was the only time that I ever had a legal right to pick a lock as part of my investigative work.

BREAKING AND ENTERING

Now, this is one of those passages you should read several times: *do not pick locks or break into places where you are not permitted or don't belong*. Now, once you have read that no less than five times, go back and read it ten more times. By this time you should start getting the picture. Not only is it just plain wrong, it is illegal. If you are caught, you may go to jail, and you will lose your license and probably never get it back.

If that's not enough, there are several other reasons why you should never commit the crime of breaking and entering (B & E). First, if you are working a case in which the information you gather is to be used in court, consider how you will be able to show it without telling everyone how you got it. Don't think for a minute that the other side will not figure it out. Even when you don't do it, you are often accused of it, so don't give them any ammunition. If you have operated illegally, even if it cannot be proven, what you have done will be known. Word of your character will circulate among those who pay you. You will only be hired by those who don't care about character. You will be paid accordingly (i.e., not often and not well when you are paid).

If you choose to learn the art of picking locks, do it for the fun of it. Impress your family and friends. If you are ever asked to speak at a luncheon, a little lock-picking demonstration is always fun. But make sure you always let your audience know that picking locks is just something you do for fun. By the way, it can keep you up to date on what types of locks are the best to use for real security.

ELECTRONIC SURVEILLANCE

Another fun thing about being a PI is that you get to spy on people. Most real PIs do this legally. Of course, if you watch TV and the movies, PIs have all kinds of toys and gadgets for listening to telephone conversations, hearing through walls, and even receiving information off their computers or fax machines. Although these things are fun, they are illegal. If you are intercepting any kind of communication via any device other than the unaided ear, it is almost always illegal. As with picking locks and B & E, you can and will go to jail if caught.

As with picking locks, knowing how to bug phones and intercept communications can be beneficial. Debugging is big business, and to know how to fight something, you have to know how it works. A long time ago (early 1960s) there were PIs in business just to do electronic eavesdropping. They would bug phones to catch cheating spouses, conduct industrial espionage, and, in some cases, get dirt on someone for blackmail purposes. In the last example, the private detective was not necessarily the one doing the blackmailing but acted as a tool of the blackmailer. This all changed with the passage of federal and state laws in the late 1960s.

Yes, there are still people in the private spy business using modern technology to snoop on people. In magazines and catalogs across the country you can buy how-to books and equipment for implementing all aspects of electronic eavesdropping. As far as I know, the First Amendment still gives us the right to *know* how to do these things, but it doesn't permit us to *use* that information to commit illegal acts. In most places, it is not even illegal to own most of the equipment needed to do the bugging. This is not an absolute, though. If you have the equipment in your house and you just enjoy playing with it, most of the time no one is going to bother you. But if you have this same equipment in a black bag and you just happen to be in the telephone room of an office building and get caught, it is a sure bet the authorities will try to put you away for a while.

So if you want to learn how to bug phones, rooms, and so on, fine. Again, knowing how it is done helps you detect it. As a private detective, you may be asked to investigate a situation where information is being stolen or intercepted. Although debugging is an art and a science in itself, having a basic knowledge will help you determine when it's time to bring in the specialist. Also, if in the course of an investigation you come across a bug, the same basic knowledge will afford you a better chance of recognizing it and determining what to do next. Be aware, though, that if you are asked to do electronic countersurveillance, the bugger may be a law enforcement agency. If you should discover that this is the case, do not touch any devices, seek counsel of an attorney immediately, and reassess your relationship with your client.

As a private detective, I have had numerous people call me and ask me to bug their phones. In less than three seconds of their asking me this I tell them no, and I tell them why. In my state, the law requires all-party consent. That is, for a conversation to be intercepted or recorded legally, all those involved must be aware that it is being intercepted or recorded. To record or intercept a conversation without the knowledge and consent of all parties involved is illegal. Private citizens and private detectives have gone to jail for doing so. Sometimes callers will tell me that they have already tapped their own phone and want some further assistance with the problem, which is usually a suspected cheating spouse. In such cases, I tell them that what they are doing is illegal and warn them that they may end up in jail if discovered. I usually follow with the suggestion that they discontinue the illegal activity and seek legal counsel. Their problem is deeper than what can be solved by simply spying on someone.

Electronic eavesdropping would appear to be one of those fun things about being a PI. And it can be a profitable business if you learn to *detect* rather than *do*. I will note here that in my experience, when clients have come to me for help because they suspected that they were being bugged they almost always were not. In some cases, though, the potential was there. In domestic cases, people will try to do anything, and with the availability of equipment at local electronics shops, it is easy to do. These types of devices are also easy to detect. They can almost always be detected visually and do not require some super-snooping electronic device.

In the cases that are not domestic, the PI must ask, "Why would anyone bug this person?" I have come across a number of people who felt the entire government, from the local to the state and federal agencies, was reading all of their mail, bugging their phones, and sending radio waves into their homes. Some of these people will, in the beginning, appear to have a legitimate problem that they want to discuss, but shortly it will become apparent that their problems are a little closer to home. For whatever reason, there are people who have been pushed over the edge psychologically and feel that their every move is being watched. Whenever you are discussing cases with potential clients, make it clear from the beginning that until you are retained you have no loyalties to them and that (in most states) they have no legal protection of confidentiality as with attorney/client privilege. And if you are retained, make it clear to your clients that if they engage in illegal behavior at any time, you may end the contractual relationship and report them to whatever authorities you deem necessary. (More on this later.)

But back to the question, "Why would anyone bug this person?" or "What makes this person so important that someone would spend the money and energy to bug him or her?" Most of the time these people can't give you any reason. Sometimes these people will tell you that they have written a number of letters to editors, local public officials, state representatives, senators, and even the president, and feel that they are being retaliated against. In these cases, they may request that you check for bugs and help them confirm their suspicions.

Every private detective handles such situations differently. Some of my associates have told people to put aluminum foil in their hats so that the radio waves will bounce off when they go out. Some have advised them to put their telephones inside a pyramid because the pyramid's energy will stop the phone from being bugged. In some cases, suggestions like these are all these people need. In most cases, the PIs I know write off this type of thing and don't charge for it.

There will be some clients who are a little more aware and will insist that something electronic must be done. For these people, a visual check, an electronic check with a simple debugging device, and installation of a surveillance block on the telephone line will usually satisfy them. Even though there is no surveillance and no devices will be found, these people will feel better only when they spend a little money. Of course, this is only done if the client has the finances to pay for such work and equipment.

Then there will be those who, no matter what you say or do, will make you part of the conspiracy against them. Try to learn to recognize them quickly. If you do a search for them and find nothing, they will not believe you. At that point, you too become a suspect. In handling people like this, understand right away that they are going to be offended at some point. It is better to get it over with as soon as possible. With tact, you can either tell them that you do not believe anything is happening and that their hiring you would be a waste of time and money, or you can just say that you are too busy and refer them to one of your associates. Your friends will appreciate the business and get you back someday. Sincerely, though, you probably will not be able to change their minds. If at any point they become threatening, which is possible, end the conversation and remind them that they are not a client yet and that you are not bound by any confidentiality. And, again, make it clear that if they do anything that is illegal or harmful to someone, you will report them to the proper authorities. Learn to deal with these kinds of people quickly. It's just part of being in business.

It is possible that someone who appears to be paranoid or neurotic could actually be the subject of electronic surveillance. But remember, there should be a reason why. How much time you spend with people who may or may not have a legitimate problem is always a judgment call. Only after years of listening to people telling you their problems are you likely to develop an "ear" for separating reality from fantasy. But remember that even in fantasy there can be a bit of truth, and sometimes it is that truth that may require further investigation.

CAR CHASES

Let's move on to the great car chases you see all the time on TV and in the movies. In reality, it's really very simple: car chase = injuries, possibly death. Most of what you do as a PI will never even remotely justify driving recklessly and endangering not only your own life but the lives of others as well. Your work can be exciting, but it is not likely that a true, life-threatening situation would arise that would require you to risk the well-being of others. It is probable that if you were to attempt to pursue a subject in a high-speed chase, there would be consequences. These might include accidents with or without injuries, speeding tickets, and property damage, as well as criminal and civil liabilities. These could cause you to lose your license and end up costing you more money than you can imagine if you are investigated by licensing authorities.

The high-speed chases you see on TV and in the movies are just to entertain you. Obviously, these are performed by professional stunt people who have special cars and equipment and are operating under controlled conditions. If nothing else, think of the last time you heard on the TV news about a high-speed chase involving a PI. It is probable that you never have and never will. And if you do, look again—it's probably on a movie or TV show that incorporates a newscast into the story.

● ● ● ● ●

Most of what was discussed in this chapter deals with some of the biggest misconceptions about PIs. TV and movies depict PIs doing many things that are not only illegal but unethical and just plain wrong. In the beginning, these very misconceptions may have been what drew you into the trade.

By now you should have seen that there are other exciting aspects of being a private detective. You don't have to break into offices to get information. You just have to work harder. And when you do, you will stand taller in the knowledge that you have done the job with the highest standards and ethics. You don't have to be macho and drive recklessly to save a life. You can save a life simply by helping people get their lives on track, helping someone who is innocent get a fair trial, providing information that will settle a civil dispute fairly, or reuniting relatives or friends who have not seen each other in years, maybe decades.

The private detective who obeys the law will eventually achieve not only business success but personal success and satisfaction. Those who do not may reap momentary financial rewards but lose in the end. If you don't get it by now, you probably never will.

CONCLUSION: MY PERSONAL MESSAGE TO YOU

This is the conclusion to this book and course of study, and with it comes a commencement—a time to celebrate the successful completion of a training program. You have not only taken steps on a journey but climbed the first of many pinnacles. From here you can begin to see many more to climb that will take you higher. The path will not be easy, but with each step, your journey will be more complete. Eventually, you will reach your goal. But before this goal is finally realized, you will see more challenges, which will require you to set new goals and demand even more from yourself. Becoming a private detective is a worthy goal and one of which to be proud. But it is just one goal.

Make it your goal to be not just a private detective, but the best private detective you can possibly be. Look for new things that will enhance your vocation. Build on what you already know in order to become even better. Become a better business person than your competition. Provide service over and above that for which you are paid. Be better than the rest.

Now comes your commencement, which means that you are about to commence this leg of your journey. You will continue on from here. As a licensed private detective myself, I too continue on a journey. Like others, I am taking steps on new paths, as should you. When I first became a private detective, I too had more to learn. Over the years, with the help of friends, family, and other PIs, I have learned new skills, gained new insights, and above all, become a better investigator. I am sure that those of you who have earnestly and sincerely followed this course of study will have already seen some differences in yourself.

My success was not immediate. You may or may not succeed in becoming a PI right away. Maybe it will take a number of attempts before you finally succeed. You may even find that being a PI isn't what you thought it would be and decide to work toward something else. Good for you. At least you are making yours a life worth living.

Remember, I wrote this book especially for you. You ask, what does it take to become a PI? I have answered that question as best I can at this time. I want you to succeed. The world will need more independent private investigators. People willing to do what the police are unwilling or unable to do. People who will come to the aid of the public to ensure a fair judicial system. People willing to do things no other sane person is likely to be willing to do. You are the person who is willing to do not just what is adequate but rather what is necessary to do the job right. You, the private detective.

With my most sincere best wishes, good luck.

—Roger J. Willard, PI

APPENDIX:

Licensing Agencies and Requirements

Remember, there is no national licensing agency for private detectives; hence, regulation is left to state, county, and local governments. The following is a brief summary of the laws, regulations, procedures, and fees involved in becoming a licensed private detective in different states. Note that it is possible in some states to have a private detective business without actually being licensed.

This list is not meant to be all-inclusive or comprehensive. It is up to you, the reader, to investigate fully all regulations involving licenses, permits, and zoning that may be applicable where you set up your business. Even as this book is being written, it is possible that the laws in your area may be changing. The only definitive sources of all of the laws, regulations, procedures, and fees that apply to you in becoming a licensed PI are the current statute books for your state, county, and municipality.

ALABAMA: A revenue-raising business license is required. For more information, contact the Office of the Attorney General, 432 Jefferson Street, Montgomery, AL 36130.

ALASKA: Alaska does not regulate private detectives. You must obtain a business license and comply with laws regarding commerce. For more information, contact the Alaska Department of Commerce and Economic Development, P.O. Box D, Juneau, AK 99811.

ARIZONA: Minimum age is 18. Three years of investigative experience required. $2,500 surety bond. $180 application fee. $300 licensing fee. For more information contact the Department of Public Safety, Licensing Section, 2102 West Encanto Blvd., P.O. Box 6638, Phoenix, AZ 85005.

ARKANSAS: Minimum age is 25. Surety bond required. For more information, contact the Attorney General, Little Rock, AR 72203.

CALIFORNIA: Minimum age is 18. Two years' related experience required. Written examination. $2,500 bond. For more information, contact the Department of Consumer Affairs, Bureau of Collection and Investigative Services, 1920 Twentieth Street, Sacramento, CA 95814.

COLORADO: Colorado has no statute requiring licensing of private detectives. For more information, contact the Attorney General, 110 Sixteenth Street, 10th Floor, Denver, CO 80202.

CONNECTICUT: Minimum age is 25. Five years' related experience required. $10,000 bond. For more information, contact the State Police Special Service Unit, Building 9, 294 Colony Street, Meriden, CT 06450.

DELAWARE: Minimum age is 25. Three years' experience as an investigator or police officer required. $45 fingerprint fee. $200 licensing fee. $300,000 liability insurance. $5,000 bond. For more information, contact the Board of Examiners for Private

Detectives, Delaware State Police, P.O. Box 430, Dover, DE 19903.

DISTRICT OF COLUMBIA: Minimum age is 18. No experience required. $5,000 bond. $158 licensing fee allows up to two people to be listed on one license. License is good for one year, from November 1 through October 31 of the next year. For more information, contact the Security Officers' Management Branch, Metropolitan Police Department, Reeves Building, 2000 14th Street N.W., 3rd Floor, Washington, D.C. 20009.

FLORIDA: Minimum age is 18. Two years of related experience or training in investigations required. $40 application fee. $50 licensing fee. $300 license fee for required agency office. $300,000 liability insurance. For more information, contact the Florida Department of State, Division of Licensing, City Center Building, 227 North Bronough Street, Tallahassee, FL 32301.

GEORGIA: Minimum age is 18. Two years of related experience required. $10,000 bond. For more information, contact the State Board of Private Detectives and Security Agencies, 166 Pryor Street, S.W., Atlanta, GA 30303.

HAWAII: Four years of related experience required. Written examination. $5,000 bond. For more information, contact the Board of Private Detectives and Guards, Department of Commerce and Consumer Affairs, P.O. Box 541, Honolulu, HI 96809.

IDAHO: The state of Idaho does not require licensing of private detectives. Some counties may have ordinances requiring licensing and bonding. For more information, contact the County Sheriff's Office or the Office of the Attorney General, Boise, ID 83720.

ILLINOIS: Minimum age is 21. Three years of related experience required. Written examination. $5,000 bond. For more information, contact the Department of Professional Regulation, Licensing Section, 320 West Washington St., Springfield, IL 62786.

INDIANA: Minimum age is 21. Two years of investigative or law enforcement experience or educational equivalent required. $100,000 liability insurance. $7,000 bond. $150 licensing fee. For more information, contact Private Detective Licensing Board, 100 North Senate Ave., Room 1021, Indianapolis, IN 46204.

IOWA: Minimum age is 18. Written examination. Liability insurance required. For more information, contact the Office of the Attorney General, State Capitol, 1007 East Grand Ave., Des Moines, IA 50319.

KANSAS: Minimum age is 21. Oral and written examination. $10,000 bond or liability insurance. $120 licensing fee. For more information, contact the Kansas Bureau of Investigation, 1620 Tyler, Topeka, KS 66612.

KENTUCKY: There are no state statutes applying to the licensing of private detectives. For more information, contact the Office of the Attorney General, The Capitol, Frankfort, KY 40601.

LOUISIANA: A revenue-raising business license may be required. For more information, contact the Office of the Attorney General, The Capitol, 900 Riverside Street N, Baton Rouge, LA 70804.

MAINE: Minimum age is 18. High school diploma plus one year experience as a police officer or investigator or six years combined experience and education required. Written examination. $10,000 bond. $200 licensing fee. For more information, contact Maine State Police, Licensing Division, State House Station #35, Augusta, ME 04333.

MARYLAND: Minimum age is 25. Five years' experience as a police officer or three years' experience as a detective or investigator required. $3,000 bond. $400 licensing fee. For more information, contact the Department of Public Safety and Correctional Services, Maryland State Police, Licensing Division (Security Annex), 1711 Belmont Ave., Woodlawn, MD 21244.

MASSACHUSETTS: Minimum age is 21. Three years' experience as an investigator or police officer of a rank higher than patrolman required. $5,000 bond. $1,100 license fee. For more information, contact the Department of Public Safety, McCormack State Office Building, 1 Ashburton Place, Boston, MA 02108.

MICHIGAN: Minimum age is 25. High school diploma and three years' experience as an investigator or police officer or college degree in police administration required. $100 license fee. $5,000 bond. For more information, contact the Michigan State Police, Private Security and Investigator Section, 7150 Harris Drive, Lansing, MI 48913.

MINNESOTA: Minimum age is 18. Three years' experience as an investigator or police officer required. $10,000 bond. Liability insurance. For more information, contact Executive Director, Minnesota

Private Detective and Protective Agent Services Board, 1246 University Ave., St. Paul, MN 55104.

MISSISSIPPI: There are no state laws concerning the licensing of private detectives. A privilege tax is required to operate a business, and, once obtained, it will permit you to work throughout the state. At this time, though, there is a strong effort to get the state to enact statewide licensing and regulations.

MISSOURI: Private detectives are regulated at the local level. For more information, contact the local city hall or the Office of Attorney General, P.O. Box 899, Jefferson City, MO 65102.

MONTANA: Minimum age is 21. High school diploma and three years' experience as a police officer or investigator required (half of the required experience may be satisfied by applicable education). Completion of a certification program. Written examination. $25,000 liability insurance. $75 licensing fee. For more information, contact the Board of Private Security Patrolmen and Investigators, Office of the Attorney General, 215 North Sanders, Justice Building, Helena, MT 59620.

NEBRASKA: Minimum age is 21. $10,000 bond. For more information, contact the Attorney General, State Office Building, 301 Centennial Mall, Lincoln, NE 68509.

NEVADA: Minimum age is 21. Five years' related experience required. Written examination. $10,000 bond. For more information, contact the Attorney General, Capitol Complex, Carson City, NV 89710.

NEW HAMPSHIRE: Minimum age is 21. $5,000 bond. For

more information, contact State Police Licenses and Permit Services, Hazen Drive, Concord, NH 03301.

NEW JERSEY: Minimum age is 21. Five years' experience as a police officer or investigator required. $3,000 bond. $250 license fee. For more information, contact the New Jersey Police, P.O. Box 70688, West Trenton, NJ 08625.

NEW MEXICO: Minimum age is 18. Three years' experience as an investigator required. $2,000 surety bond. Written examination. $200 licensing fee. For more information, contact the New Mexico Regulation and Licensing Department, Bureau of Private Investigators, Plaza San Miguel, 725 St. Michael's Dr., P.O. Box 25101, Santa Fe, NM 87504.

NEW YORK: Minimum age is 25. Two years' experience as an investigator or police officer required. Written examination. $10,000 bond. $200 licensing fee. For more information, contact the Department of State, 162 Washington Ave., Albany, NY 12231.

NORTH CAROLINA: Minimum age is 18. Written or oral examination. $50,000 liability insurance. $450 licensing fee. For more information, contact the North Carolina Private Protective Services Board, P.O. Box 29500, Raleigh, NC 27626.

NORTH DAKOTA: Minimum age is 18. Written examination. $2,500 bond. For more information, contact the Private Investigation and Security Board, P.O. Box 7026, Bismarck, ND 58507.

OHIO: Minimum age is 18. Two years' experience as an investigator or police officer with investigative duties.

$25 written examination fee. $250 license fee. $400,000 liability insurance. For more information, contact the Ohio Department of Commerce, Division of Licensing, 77 South High Street, Columbus, OH 43266.

OKLAHOMA: Minimum age is 18 to operate as an unarmed investigator and 21 years to be armed. No experience is required. State-sanctioned training of 45 hours for unarmed and an additional 20 hours for armed is required. $5,000 bond for unarmed individual and $10,000 for armed. If you have employees, $100,000 in liability insurance is required. For more information, contact Council of Law Enforcement Education Training (CLEET), P.O. Box 11476, Oklahoma City, OK 73136.

OREGON: There are no state laws concerning the licensing of private detectives. Individual municipalities may require a business license or registration with a local law enforcement agency. Private security providers are licensed by the state. For more information, contact the Attorney General, 100 Justice Building, 1162 Court St. N.E., Salem, OR 97310.

PENNSYLVANIA: Minimum age is 21. Three years' experience as an investigator or a police officer above the rank of patrolman required. $10,000 surety bond. $200 licensing fee. Licensing is through county courts. For more information, contact your county's clerk of courts.

RHODE ISLAND: There are no state laws concerning the licensing of private detectives. Individual municipalities may require licensing. For more information, contact the Attorney General, State Capitol, 101 Smith St., Providence, RI 02903.

SOUTH CAROLINA: Minimum age is 18. Two years' experience as an investigator or police officer. $225 licensing fee. $10,000 bond. For more information, contact the South Carolina Law Enforcement Division, 4400 Broad River Road, P.O. 21398, Columbia, SC 29221.

SOUTH DAKOTA: There are no specific licensing procedures or requirements. For more information, contact the Office of the Attorney General, 500 East Capitol, Pierre, SD 57501.

TENNESSEE: Minimum age is 21. Three years' experience as an investigator or law enforcement officer. $300,000 liability insurance. $100,000 property damage insurance. For information, contact the Commissioner of Commerce and Insurance, 450 James Robertson Parkway, Nashville, TN 37243.

TEXAS: Minimum age is 21. Written examination. $10,000 bond. For more information, contact the Attorney General, State Capitol, 100 East 11th St., Austin, TX 78701.

UTAH: The state of Utah does not issue licenses. Licenses must be obtained from the county or city where service is provided. For more information, contact the Department of Public Safety, 4501 South 2700 West, Salt Lake City, UT 84119.

VERMONT: Two years' experience as an investigator or police officer. Written examination. $25,000 bond. $70 licensing fee. For more information, contact Vermont Board of Private Investigative and Security

Services, Pavilion Office Building, Montpelier, VT 05602.

VIRGINIA: For information, contact the Attorney General, Supreme Court Building, 101 North 8th St., Richmond, VA 23219.

WASHINGTON: There are no state licensing laws for private detectives. Local business licenses may be required. For more information, contact Washington Department of Licensing, 1125 Washington St., S.E., Olympia, WA 98504.

WEST VIRGINIA: Three years' experience as a police officer or one year of training or experience as an investigator. $2,500 bond. $50 licensing fee. For more information, contact the Office of the Secretary of State, Room 157, State Capitol Building, Charleston, WV 25305.

WISCONSIN: $72 written examination fee. $2,000 bond or liability insurance. $50 licensing fee. For more information, contact the Department of Regulation and Licensing, P.O. Box 8935, Madison, WI 53708.

WYOMING: Minimum age is 18. $2,000 bond. For more information, contact the Office of the Attorney General, State Capitol, 100-200 West 24th St., Cheyenne, WY 82002.

RESOURCES

Butterworth Publishers
225 Wildwood Ave.
Woburn, MA 01801

Delta Press, Ltd.
215 South Washington St.
P.O. Box 1625
El Dorado, AR 71731

Eden Press, Inc.
P.O. Box 8410
Fountain Valley, CA 92728

NIC, Inc. Law Enforcement Supply
220 Carroll St., Suite D
P.O. Box 5950
Shreveport, LA 71135-5950

Nightingale-Conant Corporation
7100 North Lehigh Ave.
Niles, IL 60714
(audio tapes on personal development)

Paladin Press
P.O. Box 1307
Boulder, CO 80306

PI magazine
755 Bronx Dr.
Toledo, OH 43609

Survival Books
11106 Magnolia Blvd.
North Hollywood, CA 91601-3810

Thomas Publications
P.O. Box 33244
Austin, TX 78764

BIBLIOGRAPHY

BOOKS

Langford, M.J. *Basic Photography*, New York: Focal/Hasting House, 1977.

———. *Advanced Photography*. New York: Focal Press, 1980.

Levinson, Jay Conrad. *Guerrilla Marketing*. Boston: Houghton Mifflin Company, 1984.

———. *Guerrilla Marketing Attack*. Boston: Houghton Mifflin Company, 1989.

Mackay, Harvey. *Swim with the Sharks without Being Eaten Alive*. New York: William Morrow and Company, 1988.

Mackay, Harvey. *Beware the Naked Man Who Offers You His Shirt*. New York: William Morrow and Company, 1990.

Rice, Craig S. *Marketing without a Marketing Budget*. Holbrook, MA: Bob Adams, Inc., 1989.

Robbins, Anthony. *Unlimited Power*. New York: Fawcett Columbine, 1986.

Schwartz, David Joseph, Ph.D. *The Magic of Thinking Big.* New York: Simon and Schuster, 1987.

Sinetar, Marsha. *Do What You Love, The Money Will Follow.* New York: Paulist Press, 1987.

Withgott, Coleen K. and Austin G. Anderson. *Webster's Legal Secretaries Handbook.* Springfield, MA: Merriam-Webster, 1981.

Ziglar, Zig. *See You at the Top.* Gretna, LA: Pelican Publishing Company, 1975.

————. *Zig Ziglar's Secrets of Closing the Sale.* New York: Berkley Books, 1985.

————. *Top Performance.* New York: Berkley Books, 1987.

AUDIO TAPES

Nightingale, Earl. *Lead the Field.* Chicago: Nightingale-Conant, 1986.

————. *The Strangest Secret.* Chicago: Nightingale-Conant, 1988.